Vocabulary at the Core

Teaching the Common Core Standards

Amy Benjamin
John T. Crow

Eye On Education
6 Depot Way West, Suite 106
Larchmont, NY 10538
(914) 833–0551
(914) 833–0761 fax
www.eyeoneducation.com

Library of Congress Cataloging-in-Publication Data

Benjamin, Amy, 1951–
Vocabulary at the core : teaching the common core standards /
Amy Benjamin, John T. Crow.
     p.   cm.
ISBN 978-1-59667-211-6
1. Vocabulary—Study and teaching—United States.
2. Education—Standards—United States.
I. Crow, John T.
II. Title.
LB1574.5.B457 2011
372.44—dc23   2011043009

Sponsoring Editor: Lauren Davis
Contributing Editor: Lesli J. Favor, Ph.D.
Designer and Compositor: Matthew Williams, click! Publishing Services
Cover Designer: Dave Strauss, 3FoldDesign

Also Available from EYE ON EDUCATION

About the Authors

Amy Benjamin taught English for more than thirty years in New York. As a specialist in literacy education, she is a consultant for the National Council of Teachers of English and has worked with educators throughout the United States. Amy has been recognized for excellence in teaching by the New York State English Council, Tufts University, and Union College. Her professional goal is to help teachers in all subject areas to infuse vocabulary, reading comprehension, and writing-to-learn activities into their pedagogy. This is Amy's tenth book for Eye On Education.

John T. Crow received his Ph.D. in Curriculum and Instruction from The University of Texas at Austin. He has taught ESL, English composition, and applied linguistics courses for more than thirty years. He is a consultant for the National Council of Teachers of English and has given workshops across the United States. He is keenly interested in applying what we know about the natural learning ability of the human brain to instructional efforts in the ELA classroom.

Free Downloads

The figures displayed in this book can be downloaded and printed out by anyone who has purchased this book. Book buyers have permission to download and print out these Adobe Acrobat documents.

You can access these downloads by visiting Eye On Education's website: www.eyeoneducation.com. Click on FREE Downloads. Or search or browse our website from our home page to find this book and then scroll down for downloading instructions.

You'll need your book-buyer access code: VAC-7211-6.

Index of Downloads

Figure 4.2. Receptive vs. Productive Chart 38
Figure 4.3. Vocabulary Processing Chart 39
Figure 4.4. Blank Keyword Map 46
Figure 7.5. Math/Science Polysemes. 77
Figure 8.1. Unknown Word Chart 88

Contents

About the Authors v
Free Downloads vii
Introduction xiii
User's Guide xvii

1 Vocabulary at the Core 1
Gateways 1
Vocabulary and Education 3
Definitions Are Not Enough 3
Vocabulary at the Core 4
Not Just for English Class 5
Giving Vocabulary the Time It Deserves 7

2 What Do You Know When You "Know" a Word? 8
What Do You Know? 8
   Derivations 9
   CLASSROOM APPLICATIONS 11
      Activity 1: Group Fill-In 11
      Activity 2: Noun-Making Suffixes: Transforming Adjectives and Verbs
         into Nouns 11
   Collocations 12
   CLASSROOM APPLICATIONS 13
   Connotations 15
   CLASSROOM APPLICATION 15
   Register 16
   CLASSROOM APPLICATION 16
   Idioms 17
   CLASSROOM APPLICATION 17
   Opposites 17
   CLASSROOM APPLICATION 18
   Gender 18
   CLASSROOM APPLICATION 18
   Intentions 18
   CLASSROOM APPLICATION 18
   Conclusion 19

3   What Words Do We Teach? 20

Word Selection 21

Generic Academic Vocabulary 23

  Frequency of Occurrence 26

  CLASSROOM APPLICATIONS 26

    Implicit Instruction 26

    Explicit Instruction 27

      Classify 28

      Build 28

      Analyze 28

    Two Activities 30

      Discern 31

  Changing the Form 31

Conclusion 32

4   Receptive vs. Productive Vocabulary 33

Definitions 33

  CLASSROOM APPLICATION 36

What's Wrong with This Picture? 39

  Quiz 41

  CLASSROOM APPLICATION 43

The Keyword Map 45

Conclusion 47

5   Brain-Based Vocabulary Learning 48

Natural Learning 48

  Nonpermanent Natural Learning 48

  Permanent Natural Learning 49

  Natural vs. Rote Learning 51

The Learning Brain 51

  CLASSROOM APPLICATION 53

Conclusion 54

6   How Words Stay Learned 55

Vocabulary as Entry Points to Knowledge 55

Words as Concepts 56

  Birdiness 57

  What We Mean by Word Concepts 57

  CLASSROOM APPLICATION 58

Receptive vs. Productive Revisited 59

  Pronunciation 59

CLASSROOM APPLICATIONS 60
Spelling. 61
Other Considerations 62
CLASSROOM APPLICATIONS 64
Think-Pair-Share 64
Graphic Organizers. 64
Vocabulary Games, Puzzles, Wordplay .65
Maintenance. 65
Conclusion 66

7   Depth of Processing:
The Key to Durable Vocabulary Learning. .67
Depth of Processing Research 67
Instructional Implications 69
CLASSROOM APPLICATIONS 70
Demonstration: Shallow Processing vs. Deep 74
"The New" Bloom's Taxonomy and Depth of Processing[2] 74
Conclusion 79

8   Guessing from Context 80
Word Curiosity. 80
Context 81
How Many Unknown Words Are Too Many?. 81
Dictionaries. 84
Contextual Clues 84
Modeling. 86
CLASSROOM APPLICATIONS 87
Conclusion 89

9   Assessment 90
Receptive vs. Productive Control 91
Receptive Control 91
Productive Control 92
Shallow vs. Deep 93
About Formative and Summative Assessment. 93
Formative Assessment 94
Involving Students in Assessment 95
Do Students Actually Retain and Use Their New Words? 96
Assessment for Strategy. 97
Summative Assessments 97
Conclusion 98

Appendix A: Generic Academic Vocabulary 99
Appendix B: Latin and Greek Word Components 107
Appendix C: Shallow vs. Deep Processing. 113
Shallow Processing 113
Deeper Processing 113
Appendix D: Vocabulary Quizzes 119
Appendix E: Phrasal Verbs and Their Latinate Counterparts. 121
Appendix F: Model Activity for Vocabulary Expansion: Let's Get Kids
        Talking About Words. 125
Appendix G: Anchor Activities for Vocabulary Development. 129
Appendix H: Frequency of Occurrence 133
Appendix I: Correlation to the Common Core 135
Works Cited 149

Introduction

What if you didn't know the meaning of any of the words on this page? Half of them? One-fourth of them? Vocabulary is obviously a core skill for reading. But there is even more to this picture: Vocabulary is the way we acquire, and then access, new knowledge. And it is via vocabulary that we pass it on to others!

Vocabulary is not only the stuff of language—it is, arguably, the stuff of thought itself. Without adequate vocabulary, our students, especially those whose background knowledge does not coincide with what they need to know in school, cannot hope to succeed. And although teaching vocabulary is assumed to take place primarily in English class, vocabulary is, in fact, a core skill for *all* classes as we prepare our students for college and the business/professional world.

What does the phrase "teaching vocabulary" evoke in your mind? We're guessing that you picture lists, dictionaries, homework assignments, sentences, fill-in-the-blank tests. Such trappings are all in service to the academic tradition called "teaching vocabulary." Teachers, especially English teachers, are expected—by students, by parents, by administrators, by boards of education—to preside over lists of academic-sounding words that are called, redundantly enough, "vocabulary words." The very expression "vocabulary words" should have long ago given us some insight that something is amiss: Traditionally, we behave as if the words that we would like our students to learn are somehow set apart from their vocabulary, as though these are a set of words that live outside the collection of words that we expect them to use to communicate, to access concepts, to facilitate thought, to make sense of the world. In fact, that's pretty much what happens, or what fails to happen, as a result of our traditional vocabulary "program."

I (Amy) remember, with a mixture of amusement and frustration, "helping" my son Mitchell study for one of the weekly vocabulary tests regularly given throughout his K–12 education. He was probably in the late years of middle school or early years of high school when the scene that I have in my head played out. Now, Mitchell, like most teenagers, was not inclined to ask Mom for help with his schoolwork. But I, as an English teacher, was eager to offer what I thought should be a welcome helping hand. In any case, I was to be given the privilege of playing Mom the Vocabulary Helper only under certain constraints.

"Just ask me the words," Mitchell said evenly. "In order."

The first of the words was . . . I don't know . . . let's say it was the word "abet," meaning "to assist in a nefarious endeavor." I'd try to bring forth his background knowledge: "Did you ever hear the expression 'to aid and abet'? Like, you know, to be an accomplice to a crime? Do you know what an accomplice is?"

And he'd make a face. "Mom, just ask me the word. I don't have time for stories. I don't need to know any stories about the words. Just the definitions. C'mon. Ask me them in order. You'll see I know them."

So he would recite the definitions just as they appeared on his worksheet. If he didn't understand the words in the definitions, that was no matter because the teacher had promised not to pull any fast ones by changing the canned definitions on the Friday test. If he didn't know how the word fit into his schema, how it morphed into its various forms, how its connotation differed from its denotation, its synonyms, antonyms, nuances, that was none of his concern. I played along, grateful, in my motherly way, for the chance to spend a bit of quality time with this teenager who appeared to be needing me less and less as he relentlessly grew up.

When Mitchell came home from school after that particular test, on a Friday (of course), I asked him how he thought he had done. "It was easy," he said. And when he got his grade of 100 percent, or close to it, he was vindicated. "I told you I knew how to study."

I don't think that my son is too much different from the way my own students were in the early years of my teaching career when I used commercial vocabulary programs. As a young teacher, I didn't feel confident enough to step out from the paradigm: Give the students a list of "vocabulary words." The list often consisted of words plucked from assigned literature because, so it went, how can they comprehend *The Raven* unless they look up every word in it that they don't know? Often, the list was a weekly parade of unrelated words set forth in a workbook. It was a convenient, well-organized system, with students being introduced to this week's hit parade on Monday and then doing fill-in exercises for homework during the week. We'd visit the words at one or two points in the subsequent days of the week, perhaps "going over" the homework or grabbing a few minutes here and there to romance a matching column or "using them in a sentence." And on Friday, the test. Every few weeks, there'd be a "cumulative test."

That's how it went and no one complained. The students did well, just as Mitchell had done well, on the commercially prepared tests. They and their parents were happy. Their vocabulary grades tended to "pull up" their composition and reading comprehension grades, and the words that they "learned" were certainly outside the scope of their conversational vocabulary. Why would anyone seek to improve or change such a time-honored, well-controlled system? Who could find fault with it?

Well, as you might imagine, we do. We do find fault, and plenty of it, with the vocabulary pedagogy described above. As you've probably noticed, traditional vocabulary instruction leads to rote memorization but not true vocabulary growth. True vocabulary growth—where students *understand and use* the words that they've learned—requires two experiences that traditional workbook-like vocabulary instruction does not provide. These two experiences are (a) extensive processing of the word's meaning and use and (b) generous opportunities to use new words for meaningful communication. Add to this recipe the teacher's understanding about natural language acquisition, and you will have students whose vocabulary actually grows, rather than students who have memorized a bunch of words for a test, only to forget them as soon as the test is over.

We wrote this book to help teachers integrate vocabulary instruction with the language arts so that students could not only expand the scope of their vocabulary, but could develop their skills as lifelong learners of words and indulge their own innate joy about language. We believe that vocabulary learning needs to be both robust and gradual: By robust, we mean that vocabulary should have a much bigger place in the language arts class than just the weekly word list, and the learning of one word should lead to deeper understandings of related words. By gradual, we mean that the full meaning of a word, especially a complex word, should cover more territory than a sterile definition can convey. For many interesting words, meaning is gradually revealed through repeated exposure in various contexts. We also believe that words, once learned, need to stay learned. That means that our vocabulary instruction must be cumulative and recursive: we need to nurture new words by using them ourselves and by setting up learning experiences that will have students using new words, revisiting not-so-new ones.

This is an expanded and extended version of our book *Vocabulary at the Center*, © 2009. The chapters of this book fully develop the robust, gradual, cumulative, and recursive approach that we advocate. Each chapter is a combination of brain-based background/theoretical discussion and specific classroom applications that allow you to incorporate the concepts directly into your lesson plans. The chapters' integration of vocabulary instruction into the language arts—and beyond, through domain-specific vocabulary—aligns with the ideas set forth by the Common Core State Standards for English Language Arts and for Literacy in History/Social Studies, Science, and Technical Subjects. A chapter-by-chapter breakdown is given in the following **User's Guide**.

User's Guide

Chapter 1 gives you a deep look into what word knowledge is all about. You'll find that words learned in context reveal more and more about themselves each time they appear in a different sentence. And you'll find that a word's meaning is elastic, changeable, subtle, nuanced, and variable. There's more to knowing a word than the ability to parrot back a single, rigid definition when asked to do so on a test. You'll also realize that using a word in a sentence (meaningfully) requires a significant amount of knowledge. We don't just jump from being able to tell a definition to being able to use a word productively. There's a continuum of knowledge from Point A to Point B.

Chapter 2 may help you change your mind about the words—both the kinds of words and the amount—that you should be explicitly teaching. We make the case for relying heavily on a list that we're calling *Generic Academic Vocabulary* (GAV). You'll learn all about it in Chapter 2, plus various classroom activities that will allow students to process the words through meaningful use and analysis.

Chapter 3 explains the important difference between words we know because we've heard or read them and words we know because we've actually used them. The first category is called our *receptive* vocabulary; the second, our *productive* vocabulary. This chapter provides applications that will move the words along the continuum from total unfamiliarity, to receptive recognition, to productive use.

In Chapter 4 we talk about the instructional implications of how the brain learns best. When we compare the ways in which brains learn best to the ways in which many classrooms and schools operate, we often find a gap. Practices such as worksheets that are done in silence, lists of unconnected words out of context, and memorization that is unconnected to meaning are a few of the outdated practices that don't comport with the way brains like to soak up information.

Continuing within the landscape of the brain, we talk about word storage in Chapter 5. We explain how the brain operates like a file system that has all kinds of interrelated access points through which words may be retrieved.

Chapter 6 explains how words are learned and remembered through deep processing. In practical terms, that means that we need various engagements with new words, engagements that allow those new words to really make themselves at home in the brain's schema. We take you through a detailed analysis of many traditional vocabulary activities/assessments in terms of their depth of processing and the likelihood that they would result in durable learning. We also match depth of processing activities to Bloom's taxonomy.

Chapter 7 delves into the whole idea of guessing from context. We make the point that not all contexts are alike. Some sentences and surrounding text are much more revealing than others. Certain kinds of key words and punctuation need to be read as context clues.

The last chapter, Chapter 8, addresses assessment in a way that takes the subtleties of vocabulary learning into account. As we say throughout the book, we'd like to move you beyond traditional assessments that usually are capable only of a superficial reading of the extent to which a student knows a word.

The Appendices contain the following parts:

- Appendix A: A list of vocabulary commonly found in academic texts.
- Appendix B: A table of common Latin and Greek word components.
- Appendix C & D: Tasks to demonstrate the difference in retention between tasks that require shallow processing and tasks that require deep processing.
- Appendix E: A list of phrasal verbs and Latinate counterparts that sound more mature, more sophisticated.
- Appendix F: An example of an extended vocabulary activity that will enhance retention.
- Appendix G: Anchor activities for effective vocabulary instruction.
- Appendix H: An explanation of frequency of occurrence lists and how they can be used.
- Appendix I: A correlation table to help teachers and administrators match the classroom ideas in this book to the Common Core State Standards.

Vocabulary at the Core

There is a lot that we don't know about the inner workings of the brain, but one thing is certain: vocabulary forms the core of its conscious operation.

Gateways

Our brains are phenomenal machines—complex, interactive, and powerful, capable of feats that computer scientists can only dream of at the moment. Our brains are constantly bombarded by input from our senses, and from this information we form memories. Some are soon forgotten; others are stored in long-term memory, a process that, incidentally, occurs while we are asleep. However, memories are not stored as self-contained packets. Instead, as Sousa (2001, p. 50) notes, "Different parts of a memory are stored in various sites which reassemble when the memory is recalled." While recall can certainly be triggered by a smell, an image, a taste, etc., the primary key to recalling stored data is **vocabulary**. Hearing or reading a word or phrase allows you to access an incredible amount of information that you have stored about the targeted phenomenon.

To illustrate, think for a minute about *kitchen*. Just from seeing this word, you are able to easily recount the following:

- ♦ What a typical one contains
- ♦ What yours looks like: the location of the appliances, the placement and color of the cabinets, the floor covering, etc.
- ♦ The last thing that was prepared in it
- ♦ Where cups, dishes, silverware, etc. are stored in it
- ♦ What your kitchen smells like when your favorite dish is being prepared

- ♦   The dangers inherent in a kitchen
- ♦   What your parents' kitchen looked like
- ♦   Good or bad things that have happened to you in a kitchen

This list could go on and on. Again, what serves as a gateway, as an entry point to this amazingly large body of knowledge? The single word *kitchen*. And, of course, this is just one of tens of thousands of concepts that you have stored, each of which interconnects into a vast collection of information that is scattered throughout your brain.

Robert Marzano, author of *Building Background Knowledge for Academic Achievement* (2004), defines a word as ". . . the label associated with a packet of knowledge stored in permanent memory" (p. 32). These packets of knowledge are what he refers to as **background knowledge**. Richard Anderson called each collection of knowledge a **schema** (plural **schemata**). Every English-speaking person has a kitchen schema, for example. Every person's kitchen schema certainly will not contain the same details: there will be cultural differences, experiential differences, socioeconomic differences, and so forth. But the mere mention of the word *kitchen* allows each person to access his or her kitchen schema instantly. Words trigger schemata, opening doors to all kinds of stored knowledge.

Now imagine what it would be like if we humans had not developed language. We could still have the same brains, brains that were capable of learning from experience. So we could still store all of the same information about *kitchen*, but we would have no easy way to *access* this information. Without the organizing principle of vocabulary, all of the facts and experiences that we accumulated across time concerning *kitchen* would be randomly scattered across our brains as they occurred and, as a result, be rendered almost inaccessible. Obviously, the ability to communicate is certainly a very powerful advantage that language provides us humans. However, the ability to organize and access stored information is, perhaps, equally as important as the ability to communicate this information. And, again, central to this organization and access is *vocabulary*.

All of your students know what a kitchen is. They know the word *kitchen* not only because they've heard it countless times, but also because of their experiences. And they've had reason to use the word *kitchen*. Now think about a word that might appear on one of your vocabulary lists, or in a poem, or a novel, or a historical document, or a newspaper editorial—a word that your students would not know. When they hear or read such a word, nothing is triggered: no images, no familiar experiences, no cavalcade of other words associated with it. Without the ability to access the background knowledge that might be associated with this word, your students' ability to interact with the content and to interrelate it with existing information—without this gateway to previous experiences, comprehension begins to grind to a halt. If too many gateways are blocked, comprehension stops completely.

For example, what if someone came up to you and asked, "How are transposons remethylated during epigenetic reprogramming?" If you share a background similar to ours, namely, a very limited exposure to microbiology, this question would not provide a gateway to a single schema, to the slightest bit of background knowledge. Vocabulary is at the core of our ability to communicate or to absorb new knowledge.

Vocabulary and Education

Research shows over and over that vocabulary skills correlate very highly with academic ability:

- Intelligence: Anderson and Freebody note that "the strong relationship between vocabulary and general intelligence is one of the most robust findings in the history of intelligence testing" (quoted in Marzano, 2004, p. 32). Vocabulary scores correlate more highly with intelligence levels than any other individual measure. That's why standardized tests such as the SAT, ACT, and GRE have a vocabulary component.
- Reading: Farley and Elmore studied college students enrolled in remedial reading. They found that vocabulary was the *only statistically significant predictor* of various reading skills. According to Fisher and Frey (2008), research confirms that ". . . students with smaller vocabularies and lower comprehension levels read with more trepidation, question the text less, and fail to notice when they don't understand something" (p. 4).
- Predictor of Academic Success: Reading comprehension has been repeatedly shown to be a good predictor of academic success at the high school and college levels. So the chain is complete: vocabulary is an excellent predictor of reading ability, and reading ability is an excellent predictor of academic success. Vocabulary truly is at the core—not only of the ELA classroom, but in all of the content areas.

Definitions Are Not Enough

Research has consistently shown that definitional information alone does not make a significant contribution to reading comprehension. In a foundational article that synthesizes vocabulary instruction research, Baumann and Kameenui cite several studies that support the following statement: Having students learn nothing more than words and their definitions does not significantly improve reading comprehension of texts that contain the targeted words. So preparing students for a reading passage by having them memorize words + definitions that the passage contains is of very limited value, Words are not directly linked to their definitions in one's brain. They are, instead, gateways to richly interconnected information that a word holds. If that's the way that words are stored in one's brain, doesn't it make sense that that's the way we should be teaching them?

It's not that we shouldn't be teaching definitions. Of course, a definition illuminates a word's meaning. What we're saying is that teaching the definition alone—matching a word to a corresponding synonym or phrase that crystallizes its meaning—is not sufficient information. In the next chapter, you'll discover more about what it actually means to know a word.

Vocabulary at the Core

Catherine Snow, Harvard professor and researcher on adolescent literacy and author of *Preparing Our Teachers: Opportunities for Better Reading Instruction*, is a strong advocate for vocabulary development as a key means for strengthening academic success. She stresses the importance of ongoing, persistent efforts at vocabulary development at all grade levels. Snow, whose research team made detailed observations about the achievement gap in Boston schools in the early 2000s, exposes the differences in vocabulary knowledge between "middle-class kids with well-educated parents" and "kids of undereducated parents who don't talk to them very much" (Vaishnav, 2009). The disadvantaged children's vocabulary was estimated at around 4,000 words in the third grade. The more advantaged children had a vocabulary of 12,000 words. Snow concludes that organized effort to increase children's vocabulary in school as early as possible is the best way to shrink the achievement gap.

The outlook for students having a vocabulary deficit in the early grades is dismal because as they progress up the grades, two things happen to work against them:

1. They encounter an increasing number of unknown words in content area text. Lacking vocabulary to begin with, they cannot use context clues.
2. Decreasingly explicit vocabulary instruction is provided.

Vocabulary, then, is to academic learning what cardiovascular strength is to fitness. And just as most people have to go out of their way to achieve cardiovascular fitness by working out (rather than relying on their ordinary activities to build sufficient strength), educators have to be deliberate and conscious about improving students' vocabulary. Vocabulary development has to take its place at the core of the curriculum because it is foundational to all academic achievement.

Not Just for English Class

Vocabulary instruction is everybody's business. In all subject areas, students need to learn a specialized language: the language of mathematics, the language of science, the language of music, and so on. In addition to the specialized terminology that might be found in the glossary of a subject area textbook, we have a general level of language for academic conversation. Here's a sampling of the kinds of language students hear and read in high school on a typical day:

> *A square root of a nonnegative number N is one of two equal numbers whose product is N.*
>
> *Our sales forecast for the next quarter will form the basis for our financial plans for the remainder of the current fiscal year. From the sales forecast we will develop production plans.*
>
> *Molten rock, called magma, solidifies deep within the Earth. The final rock type is determined by the chemical composition of the magma and the rate at which it cooled.*
>
> *The actors in this dreadful tragedy were a party of soldiers commanded by Captain Preston of the 29th regiment. This party, including the captain, consisted of eight, who are all committed to jail.*
>
> *Verbs tell what a subject does, has, or is. The verb resides in the predicate, along with the modifiers of the verb, if there are any.*

How many of the words in these sentences would stump your students? How helpful is the context? How many words have subject-specific meanings? How many words represent abstract qualities for which your students may have no concrete association? If words unlock known information, how much of that information remains locked when the students read these sentences in academic text? Yet, while all of this unfamiliar vocabulary is paraded across the students' eyes, it's very likely that no coordination of vocabulary is going on from class to class. Opportunities to have students make connections are missed.

In *Active Literacy Across the Curriculum: Strategies for Reading, Writing, Speaking and Listening* (2006), Heidi Hayes Jacobs says:

We should be pumping our students full of words. Although teachers engage in the well-established practice of giving out vocabulary lists of words developed by English teachers for students to look up and define and use in a sentence, these words are often de-contextualized or simply lifted from ongoing literature studies. What is rare is for the words to actually be used especially in a natural context, outside of a discussion about a particular work of literature. Providing a list of enriched words that make sense for application in any given unit, posting them with the highest visibility, and then requiring their usage in assignments are key to improving student success across the curriculum. (p. 34)

To get there, we need to make academic words readily available, that is, visible. A good way to do this is to provide word walls and word banks. A word wall is simply a classroom display of key words. Here are some ways to use word walls:

1. Permanent word walls are lists of words that are staples in academic life, but that students don't ordinarily use or hear in their social conversations: *analysis, determine, represent, outcome, identify, contrast, model, analogy, metaphor*, etc. (See Appendix A: Generic Academic Vocabulary)
2. Unit word walls are the kinds of words and phrases that would be in a glossary for a particular unit. Because such words are related, unit word walls should illustrate categories, hierarchies, taxonomies. The term *semantic map* is used to refer to displays like this.
3. One-day word walls are simply a list of words on the board that will be used heavily over the course of the coming lesson or two. They focus students on key ideas.

A good word wall can consist of just a handful of words, and should not be too labor-intensive for you. Suggestion: Write your words on separate index cards, using a bold marker. That way, you will have a reusable set of words that you can rotate throughout the year.

When you have an in-class essay, consider giving students a word bank so that they can enrich their language. For example, if you wanted students to write a character sketch, your word bank might look like this:

personality traits
characteristics
relationship
development
lifestyle

Note that these words may not be unfamiliar to students, but they may be words that students are unlikely to use unless prompted. Notice also that these kinds of words will generate elevated thinking, not because they are fancy, but because they name abstract concepts.

Giving Vocabulary the Time It Deserves

I (Amy) once gave a reading comprehension workshop that had vocabulary instruction on the agenda. An English teacher's face lit up, and she said, "Oh, good. We really need that. I'm really looking for a way to get kids to remember the words. And use them. All they do is learn the words for the test." So I thought this would be a great workshop for this teacher. "Oh," I said, delightedly. "You've come to the right place."

So there I went, explaining the value of morphology charts, displaying semantic maps, talking about cross-disciplinary connections, touting the importance of etymology, sharing "word reports" that my students had written, explaining why we need to teach shades of meaning and multiple meanings of words in various contexts.

To my chagrin, the teacher who declared the need to "get kids to remember and use their vocabulary words" looked grim. "But that would take too long," she said. "I need to get through my vocabulary so I can teach writing and literature."

What we want to emphasize is that teaching vocabulary well—so that new words are understood, remembered, and used—is foundational. But we aren't being given any more time to do it. So, we have to make simultaneous use of instructional time. We need to teach words that fit right in to whatever else we are teaching so that vocabulary instruction is seen not as an "add on" but as a resource that feeds thinking. That is what we mean when we say that vocabulary is at the core.

What Do You Know When
You "Know" a Word?

So let's face it: teaching vocabulary in the traditional manner has not proven to be very successful. Students are given a list of words on Monday, asked to look them up and memorize them during the week, and given a test on Friday, a test that often includes the instruction to use some or all of the words in sentences. By the following Friday, students have "forgotten" most of the words that they "knew" the previous Friday.

One of the primary reasons for the failure of traditional vocabulary instruction is that people seriously underestimate what knowledge is necessary in order to be in total control of a word, that is, to be able to use words in sentences of your own making. Thus, we would like to begin our trip into Vocabulary Land by helping you to appreciate what native speakers know when they truly know a word—to appreciate the extent to which vocabulary truly is at the core of language. We do not present this information because you will have to teach it to your native-speaking students; we present the information to help you appreciate the complexities of vocabulary acquisition. Once you have gained an appreciation for this body of knowledge, you will better understand why past efforts at vocabulary instruction have been, for the most part, less than successful. This information will then serve as a backdrop against which we will present methods and activities that help students acquire vocabulary that, with proper exposure, lasts a lifetime. Let's get started!

What Do You Know?

If you were to ask the average person on the street what knowing a word entails, you would most likely get a list of three items:

1. Its meaning
2. Its pronunciation
3. Its spelling

(Some people might add a fourth item: How to use it in a sentence. However, knowing "how to use it in a sentence" glosses over a huge body of information, so let's hold off on that one.)

These three areas of knowledge are, obviously, critically important. But they only scratch the surface. Let's poke around a bit and see what else you know when you know a word.[1]

Derivations

When you know a word, you know how it can change. To illustrate, fill in the empty cells in Figure 2.1, thinking about the knowledge that you possess that allows you to do this task so easily. We'll do the first one for you:

FIGURE 2.1. Prefixes

Positive	*Negative*
legal	*illegal*
possible	
relevant	
appear	
divisible	
reliable	

Would it ever occur to you to say something like "You can't do that—that's disposable"? Or "That's unlegal"? Of course not—to a native speaker of English, that sounds incredibly wrong. Yet, you probably can't explain why you know that the negative form of "reliable" is "unreliable" and not "disreliable"

[1]We are referring here to the knowledge that a native speaker has about English. Nonnative speakers, even advanced ones, may very well have gaps, especially with some of the finer points.

FIGURE 2.2. Suffixes

Country	People
China	*Chinese*
Cuba	
Brazil	
Iraq	
Spain	
Germany	
France	
Holland	

or "inreliable." You produce the word "unreliable" because that's the form that you've heard repeatedly. You've come to know it intuitively.

Figure 2.1 deals with prefixes—things added to the left side of words. Now let's look at suffixes—the right side. Fill in the empty cells in Figure 2.2, concentrating on the knowledge that you possess that allows you to complete the task so easily.

Would it ever occur to you to say "He speaks Chinan" or "He speaks Cubese"? Again, the answer is obvious: of course not. Think about how your knowledge grows out of having heard the word forms that you've heard repeatedly, developing your intuition about adding suffixes.

Figure 2.1 shows six different ways to change a word from positive to negative and Figure 2.2 shows eight different ways to change from the country to the people of that country. So you can see that you already know what derivations are in English—and so do your students. They just don't use the word *derivation* to speak of the many changes that can be made to a word that they know.

Do you remember memorizing lists of this kind of stuff as a child? ("Let's see: the opposite of **appear** is **disappear**, but the opposite of **possible** is **impossible**. How can I remember that?") Again, of course not—you learned this information naturally as you were acquiring English. And these examples only represent the tip of the iceberg: The body of knowledge that you have about word derivations is immense!

CLASSROOM APPLICATIONS

Help students give themselves credit for their intuition about word derivations. By giving themselves due credit for their ability to change the forms of words that they know, students will broaden their understanding of what it is to know a word.

Activity 1: Group Fill-In

Do Figures 2.1 and 2.2 as a class activity. Tell the students that you want to help them appreciate how much they already know about English vocabulary. The steps are as follows:

♦ Present Figure 2.1 to your class orally, much in the same manner as we presented it to you in writing: Tell the class that you will give them the positive and that you want them to give you the negative. Model the activity with the first row of the table. Then read each word in the left-hand column and ask students, as a group, to give you the negative form.

♦ Introduce the term *derivation*. Tell the class that just knowing a word isn't enough: you have to know how to change words to make them fit the situation.

♦ Give them a couple of wrong derivations to let them see how silly they sound (**dispossible**, for example). Then ask them *why* the opposite of **appear** is **disappear**, but the opposite of **possible** is **impossible**. (There is no answer; derivations are often not logical.)

♦ If *prefix* is a new concept for your students, introduce it now. Tell them that this exercise has worked with prefixes, things you add to the beginning of words.

♦ If *suffix* is a new concept, introduce it now. Tell your students that you are now going to show them a bit about what they know about suffixes—things you add to the end of words. Then do Figure 2.2 in the same manner as you did Figure 2.1.

This activity takes much longer to write up than to do in class. Plan on spending between 5 and 10 minutes on the whole exercise, depending on how much discussion your questions generate.

Activity 2: Noun-Making Suffixes: Transforming Adjectives and Verbs into Nouns

The purpose of this activity is to have students understand that their ability to turn an adjective or verb into a noun creates an abstract idea. The process is simple: You list several common noun-making suffixes on the board. Meanwhile, students create a list of verbs and adjectives about a particular topic. You may use the topics such as food, music, sports, animals, or something that is related to your current readings: "Write ten verbs that tell what a character in a novel is doing; write ten adjectives that describe the character 's personality." What we're then going to do is match up these words with the noun-making suffixes, to the extent that we can. Of course, not all of the words will be able to play the role of noun by dressing in any of the "noun costumes."

Have dictionaries on hand so that students can verify whether a "nounified" word is legitimate.

The most common noun-making suffixes are *-ment, -ness, -hood, -tion (-sion), -ity, -ism, -itude, -ence, -ance, -ist, -er, -or*.

To extend this activity, you can create adjectives out of nouns and verbs with these suffixes: *-y; -ish, -al,-ive, -ful, -able, -ible, -en*. You can create verbs out of nouns and adjectives with these suffixes: *-ize, -ify*.

When students engage in this word-synthesizing activity, they become more comfortable in the realm of Latinate words, words that are commonly used for academic and business communication.

Of course, spelling must be considered when we add a suffix. (Actually, there are spelling implications involved when we add a prefix as well, but adding a prefix is a simple matter: no letters get dropped or doubled when we add a prefix.) Instead of giving the students the spelling rules, which they no doubt have heard before, have them verify spellings in a dictionary. Then, if you intend to delve into spelling patterns, have them group the words in accordance with whether they stay the same, drop a silent *e*, double the final consonant, or change a letter in the stem of the word when adding a prefix. By observing the groupings, have the students use inductive reasoning to generate a rule that describes the spelling patterns. (When students generate a rule based on their own observations about patterns, that rule is learned much more durably than when they are simply *given* the rule and asked to apply it.)

Collocations

Collocation refers to our knowledge about what words fit with each other. Why, for example, do we say a *piece of paper*? Why not a *unit, portion, section, chunk,* or *slice*? There is no logical reason—in English, we say a *piece of paper*. That's all. Exploring collocations with students teaches and expands on the Common Core Language standards for selecting and using parts of speech in standard English.

When you know a word, you know what that word goes together with—a truly *enormous* body of knowledge. Here are just a few of the thousands and thousands of examples:

FIGURE 2.3. Separateable?

Unseparated	Separated
look up the word	**look** the word **up**
look over the book	**look** the book **over**
look down on John	*look John **down on** *look **down** John **on**
look into the decision	*look the decision **into**
We use an asterisk (*) to flag sentences or phrases that are not properly formed.	

1. I _____ afford to buy a new car. (Only *can* or *cannot* fits here.)
2. solar _____ , nervous _____ , stereo _____ , digestive _____ , get it out of your _____ (Only *system* fits in all the blanks.)
3. Why can a toilet run, but a sink cannot? Why can the air conditioner be running but a toaster cannot?
4. bread and butter (never butter and bread), knife and fork, bride and groom, etc. These pairings are called *freezes*: collocations that are normally spoken in a specific order.
5. Why am I mad *at* you (not *with*, *by*, *of*, etc.)?
6. Notice what happens to the meaning when we change the combination of words with look: look up, look down on, look forward to, look in on, look like, look into, look over, look up to.

There is another "hidden" piece of knowledge that you have about verb phrases such as the ones listed in #6: you know when you can rearrange things by separating these phrases. Look at Figure 2.3 above.

●CLASSROOM APPLICATIONS

Phrasal verbs offer two important instructional implications:

1. They are vexing to English language learners.
2. They are conversational in tone.

We can address the first implication, the trouble that English language learners have with phrasal verbs, by developing the habit of self-translating as we use these phrasal verbs with students. We can also encourage them to take special

FIGURE 2.4. Phrasal Verbs and Latinate Correspondents

Phrasal Verb	*Latinate Correspondent*
make up	consist
set up	establish, institute
point out	indicate
help out	assist
end up	conclude
keep up	maintain
figure out	perceive, deduce
lock up, lock out, lock in	secure
move out, move over, switch around	transfer
give in	consent
sign up	register
leave out	exclude
line up	correspond
think up	scheme

notice of phrasal verbs that they hear in conversation. An enjoyable and productive way to do this is to ask students to watch sitcoms, listening carefully for phrasal verbs. (Because the language register of sitcoms is casual and conversational, they will hear a lot of phrasal verbs.) Have them keep a journal of two or three phrasal verbs that they hear for each sitcom, along with the context: What is the speaker trying to convey in the sentence that has the phrasal verb?

We can use this activity to elevate the language of our native speakers as well, because phrasal verbs, being conversational, usually have a Latinate correspondent; that is, for every casual phrasal verb, there's a more formal word that matches it, or that comes close, as shown in Figure 2.4.

Connotations

When you know a word, you not only know what a word actually means, you also know its connotations. You can explain connotations to students as "the emotional freight of a word," or "the feelings that you get when you hear a particular word."

1. What is the difference between "We will *eat* at 6:00" and "We will *dine* at 6:00"?
2. What is the difference between *house, home, domicile, residence, living quarters, pad, crib*? With what audience or context might you use each?

CLASSROOM APPLICATION

Have students enact a conflict, such as an argument over a parking spot or choice seat. Have them do the enactment in two ways: First, using language that is as polite and diplomatic as possible; then, using incendiary language to express the same ideas. When they plan out their words, they should concentrate on "translations" from words that have neutral or positive connotations to those that have negative connotations, rather than just adding words to spark a confrontation.

To get students to understand connotation, use variations of this theme, such as having students describe, either in writing or as a skit, an incident to different audiences for different purposes.

Scenario: You witness an "exciting" incident in the hall of your school. Describe the incident to the following people, for the following purposes:

1. You are describing the incident to your friends at lunch. Your purpose is to entertain them.
2. You are describing the incident to the dean of students. Your purpose is to protect the identities of those involved, but to reveal the whole truth of what you saw.
3. You are describing the incident to your English teacher, who has asked you to write a comparison/contrast essay about a conflict that you have seen or experienced and the conflict in the first scene of *Romeo and Juliet*. Your purpose is to demonstrate to your teacher that you can use formal academic style to compare and contrast.

Register

When you know a word, you know which words to use for a variety of audiences. Bad words are the obvious example: you have to be careful where you use them (if you do at all). Or what if one of your students came into the classroom and greeted you as follows: "Yo, teach." Or "S'up dude?"

There is, of course, a lot of overlap between **connotation** and **register**: The **connotation** of a word often determines when (in which **register**) you would use it. For example, the words that you would choose to express yourself if you were giving a professional presentation to other teachers would often be very different from the words that you would choose with your students. Register correlates to the Common Core approach to teaching spoken and written tone and style, as in the requirement to use a formal style and objective tone in a piece of writing.

●LASSROOM APPLICATION

Try any or all of the following three activities to help students understand register.

♦ Have students peruse the newspaper for a story about a conflict. (This should not be hard to find.) Have them then rewrite the story as a blog entry, using a different register. (Note that in both of these activities, the one for connotation and the one for register, the students should feel the need for a dictionary as a reference. If they don't, then chances are that they are not reaching out for new words, thus not stretching their vocabulary sufficiently to justify the activity. To avoid this, you might provide a word bank of language that you think is either unfamiliar or underused by the students.)

Going from one register to another is called code-switching. We code-switch all the time as we adjust our language register by choosing words that we think our audience expects under the circumstances. Code-switching applies to many dimensions of human interaction: how well we know a person, whether we are in public or in private, whether we are communicating with a contemporary or an older person, a coworker, or a boss, and so on.

♦ Comedy, intended or unintended, results from miscues in language register. A classroom application that engages students in language register is to have them enact a skit in which people choose words that are *inappropriate* (either too formal or too informal) for the conversation.

- Writers create characters who are adept at code-switching into different registers, just as real people are. Analyze the word choices that signal formal or informal register in characters such as Holden Caulfield, Huck Finn, and Elizabeth Bennett.

Idioms

When you know a word, you know its idiomatic uses. An idiom is a phrase whose meaning cannot be determined by looking up the individual words. Consider the difference between these two sentences:

1. John kicked the pail.
2. John kicked the bucket.

If you looked up the words in both of the above sentences, you would conclude that they mean almost the same thing. However, because of your in-depth knowledge of **pail** vs. **bucket**, you are well aware of the vast difference in meaning.

CLASSROOM APPLICATION

Let's again turn to our literature for this one. Writers put idioms in their characters' mouths all the time. The older the book is, and the more distant it is geographically from the student's own culture, the more likely we are to find unfamiliar idioms. In addition to the usual vocabulary that lurks in the literature that your students are reading, have students find idioms and research their histories. Your nearest librarian will be delighted to acquaint your students with specialized dictionaries in the reference section that offer etymologies of all kinds of idiomatic expressions.

Opposites

When you know a word, you know its opposites. However, opposites are not as obvious as you might think. Examples:

- What is the opposite of *short*? If you are talking about *height*, then the opposite is **tall**. However, if you are talking about a *movie*, then it's **long**.
- What is the opposite of *old*? If you are talking about *a person's age*, then the opposite is **young**. However, if you are talking about a *movie*, then it's **new**.

●CLASSROOM APPLICATION

As you can see from these examples, a word may have more then one opposite, depending on how it's used. How many opposites can your students think of for the following everyday words?

funny   serious   mad   nothing   work

Gender

When you know a word, you know whether it is used primarily by males or females. Although English doesn't have big gender differences at the word level, they do exist. Most men, for example, would never dream of saying, "Look at that *darling* little pillow—isn't it *precious*?"

●CLASSROOM APPLICATION

The Outsiders is a classroom staple whose female author, S.E. Hinton, created a male persona as her narrator. I've heard that some students consider the narra-tor 's voice inauthentic because they claim to be able to associate some of his language more with a female voice than with a male's.

See if your students agree.

Intentions

When you know a word, you know what the speaker intends when the speaker uses it in different ways. For example, you can change your intonation and, perhaps, your nonverbal language and mean three entirely different things when you say "hello":

1. *Neutral:* How you would say it when answering the telephone or greeting a stranger on the street.
2. *Surprise:* How you would say it if you found something by surprise. Imagine, for example, that you were looking through a stack of papers and found something that wasn't supposed to be there: "Hello! What's this doing here?"
3. *Ridicule:* How you would say it if you wanted to say "It's about time you figured that out," or, in the popular parlance, "Duh!"

●CLASSROOM APPLICATION

Go to your Shakespeare for this. Students (and many teachers) fear Shakespear-ean text, believing, wrongly, that there's nothing in it that they understand. In fact, if looked at closely, there's much more in Shakespeare that they do understand than they think. Ask them to find a short sentence—a command or a question will do nicely—and stretch its meaning by using vocal cues such as volume, stress, pitch, and pause to alter the intent of the words.

There are more areas of knowledge that we could explore if space permitted However, the ones listed here should suffice to show you that you are in control of a sizable body of knowledge when you truly "know" a word.

Of course, you're not going to include all of these lessons for each word that you want students to know. But you can use the information and classroom applications in this chapter to give students deeper understandings of how language works and what it means to know a word.

Conclusion

When we truly know a word, we know a vast, interconnected network of information about that word. In this chapter, we explored the following areas:

- ♦ Spelling
- ♦ Pronunciation
- ♦ Meaning(s)
- ♦ Derivations: how words take on prefixes and suffixes to make new forms
- ♦ Collocations: groups of words that form acceptable phrases
- ♦ Connotations: the "feelings" associated with a word
- ♦ Register: from formal to informal to slang—what words and collocations belong where
- ♦ Idioms: phrases whose meaning cannot be discerned by looking up the individual words
- ♦ Opposites
- ♦ Gender: which words or collocations sound more feminine or masculine
- ♦ Intentions: how a word can change meanings by changing intonation and gestures

As you can see, the list is quite daunting—and it's not a complete listing. At a minimum, we would have to add that facet of vocabulary that we explored in the previous chapter: words serve as a gateway to schema, to our experience and background knowledge about the world. For people to be able to fully use and understand a word, they must be in control of a truly amazing amount of knowledge. Keep this complexity in mind as we continue to explore explicit vocabulary teaching.

What Words Do We Teach?

In Chapter 2, we explored the intricacies involved with being in full control of words. The first question that might pop into your head is should we even teach vocabulary explicitly? If the body of knowledge is so complex, are we, given the time that we have available to us and the amount of material that we have to cover, just wasting our time? The answer is a very resounding "No!" Research very clearly supports the value of properly structured direct vocabulary instruction.

In *Building Background Knowledge for Academic Achievement* (2004), Robert Marzano asserts that students, especially our most needful students, need *both* implicit and explicit vocabulary instruction.

- By "implicit instruction," we mean the kind of vocabulary growth that results naturally from heavy exposure to elevated language, mostly through reading and listening, but also through the need to speak and write about subjects on one's "knowledge frontier."
- By "explicit instruction," we mean the kind of vocabulary growth that results from planned lessons designed to teach students a specific body of words.

You may hear implicit and explicit instruction referred to as indirect and direct instruction, respectively. Although Marzano acknowledges the power of implicit/indirect instruction, he also cites research that advocates for explicit/ direct vocabulary instruction: "From a number of perspectives, the research indicates that wide reading probably is not sufficient to ensure that students will develop the necessary vocabulary and consequently the necessary academic background knowledge to do well in school. In contrast, direct vocabulary instruction has an impressive track record of improving students' background knowledge and the comprehension of academic content" (p. 69). Students may gain knowledge, but it is of little value without the vocabulary to access or express this knowledge. Because vocabulary is at the core, explicit instruction makes a significant contribution to student learning.

Word Selection

A key factor in explicit vocabulary instruction is deciding which words to target. We certainly can't teach every new word that students encounter, especially in an English class, where much of their assigned literature is studded with archaic words, allusions, and what the Medieval poet John Lydgate fondly refers to as "aureate" words. These would be words that, literally translated, have a "golden hue" to them—precious gems of words, glittering with their own rarity. Take a look at two stanzas from *The Raven*, a poem that is usually presented to students in the 7 to 9 grade band:

> Once upon a midnight dreary, while I pondered, weak and weary,
> Over many a quaint and curious volume of forgotten lore,
> While I nodded, nearly napping, suddenly there came a tapping,
> As of some one gently rapping, rapping at my chamber door.
> "'Tis some visitor," I muttered, "tapping at my chamber door—
>   Only this, and nothing more."
>
> Ah, distinctly I remember it was in the bleak December
> And each separate dying ember wrought its ghost upon the floor.
> Eagerly I wished the morrow—vainly I had sought to borrow
> From my books surcease of sorrow—sorrow for the lost Lenore
> Whom the rare and radiant maiden whom the angels named Lenore
>   Nameless here for evermore.

Let's zoom in on a ninth grade teacher whom we'll call Mrs. Grover. We'll have an analytical look at the kind of instructional decisions about vocabulary she would be making in creating a list from this literature. For the first stanza, she would have *pondered* and *lore*, maybe *quaint* and *muttered*. For the second stanza, she would definitely have *ember, wrought, morrow, vainly, surcease*. She'd think about adding *bleak, sought*, and maybe even *distinctly* and *radiant*. In case you haven't noticed, the criteria that Mrs. Grover is using is the extent to which the words are unknown—their level of obscurity. The more obscure a word is, the more likely Mrs. Grover is to place it on her list because she's thinking that students must know every word in the poem in order to understand it. She's thinking that the more unfamiliar the students are with a particular word—the further away it is from their background knowledge—the more she *needs* to devote instructional time to make it accessible so that the students understand the meaning of the poem, line by line.

With only two stanzas of a much longer poem "done," she's either going to have a list with close to a hundred words on it after she completes the entire poem or some words will have to be sacrificed. Unfortunately, Mrs. Grover, like many English teachers, is going to jettison the words that are easier (those on the "maybe" list) in favor of words like *surcease, nepenthe, quaff,* and *Plutonian.*

What do Mrs. Grover's students get from her efforts? They increase their vocabulary by words that have extremely limited use. Let's face it: how much use are Mrs. Grover's students going to get from *obeisance* and *Gilead*, especially when she knows that if she asks them to *analyze* the poem, rather than *summarize* it, they will demonstrate that they don't really know the difference in meaning between the words *analyze* and *summarize.* Now *that's* a vocabulary problem that needs to be addressed! Of course, who knows? Maybe their next visit to the mall will run them smack into a sign with the word *betook* or *entreating* on it, and then wouldn't they be lucky to have learned their *Raven* vocabulary? (Please don't think that we're *never* going to address low-frequency literary, even archaic words that are the sauce to literature. We will do so *after* we take care of fundamentals that allow access to those words.)

To make matters worse, because Mrs. Grover's students rarely, if ever, come across many of these words again, this "increase" in vocabulary is quickly lost. Perhaps her students will cram the information into their brains long enough to pass her vocabulary test on Friday, but the long-term effect on their vocabulary acquisition will be practically nil. (We'll see why in future chapters.)

We can't use a shotgun approach to vocabulary, just working on words as they show up. Doing that would negate the value that Marzano speaks of when he acknowledges the importance of explicit/direct vocabulary instruction. When we teach only "words taken from the literature that we are reading," our explicit/direct instruction is hit and miss. We need an overall game plan for vocabulary instruction. We need a master list, and that master list must consist of words worth knowing because **our students will see them again and again in academic discourse**. These are the words that tend to be at the core of content area reading and discussion, and their acquisition and use contributes to students' proficiency in reading complex texts in a variety of content areas, as advocated by the Common Core State Standards.

What follows are four categories of words that can comprise your vocabulary instruction to answer the question: *What words do we teach?*

1. *The Generic Academic Vocabulary (GAV) List (see page 23):* These are words that your students will encounter frequently in academic

discourse all day long, from all of their teachers in all of their subjects. Yet, these words may not yet be fully integrated into their existing vocabulary. A heavy majority of these words have a Latinate base; some have a Greek base.

2. *Literary words:* These are the sometimes ornate, "precious gem" words that sparkle and glow in the special language of literary genres. Many of these words also have a Latinate base with a heavy French influence.

3. *Subject-specific words:* These are the kinds of words that appear in subject area glossaries. Here is where you'll find a lot of Greek-based word components.

4. *Interesting words:* These are those wonderful "relish" words that you read in well-written newspaper articles and hear in fine oratory from the mouths of speakers whose language you admire. These are the words that attract you. You want to get to know them because of their beauty, specificity, moxie, verve, and ability to do a job that might have taken you five words to do (and do less well).

Generic Academic Vocabulary

In this text, we are going to use a list of words that are given below. In Appendix A, you'll find these words with their family members (the words derived from them). We've compiled this list from several sources, including our own experience of working with students, texts used in school, and reputable newspapers and news sources, as well as academic language across the curriculum. The words that we've included are ones that are commonly used in academic and serious public discourse, but are uncommonly found in the conversations of most students in their lives outside of the classroom. We've organized the list into twelve general areas of meaning:

1. **Words that indicate the requirements of a task**—*analyze, annotate, apply, assert, assess, clarify, coherent, comment, concise, convince, critique, debate, describe, determine, discuss, dissuade, employ, espouse, estimate, evaluate, explain, extrapolate, identify, implement, interpret, overview, persuade, precise, refute, review, specify, stipulate, summary, support, thorough, well-developed, well-organized*

2. **Words that establish relationships within units of information**—*accordingly, aforementioned, afterwards, albeit, although, arguably, as follows, as such, because of, by means of, compared (to), conclusive, coupled with, decidedly, despite, due to, even so, even though, except for, foregoing,*

furthermore, greater than, hence, however, in accordance with, in conjunction with, in contrast (to), in fact, in relation to, relative to, in spite of, in this regard, inasmuch as, less than, lest, likewise, moreover, nevertheless, notwithstanding, owing to, per se, regarding, regardless, respectively, save (to mean except), set forth, similarly, such as, the following, therefore, thus, unless, whence, whereas, whereby, wherefore, wherein, with regard to, with the exception of

3. **Words about space and divisions of space**—*adjacent, area, arena, array, bilateral, continuum, dimension, external, facet, internal, intersection, lateral, linear, orientation, parameters, permeate, pervasive, precinct, proximity, realm, region, scope, section, sector, spectrum, throughout, unilateral*

4. **Words that are about how we think about a topic**—*acknowledge, assume, deductive reasoning, essential, fundamental, given (noun), imply, inductive reasoning, infer, intuition, objective, overarching, perspective, premise, process of elimination, rudimentary, subjective, tentative, theme, theory*

5. **Words about organization**—*breakdown, category, chapter, classification, complement, complex, component, compound, consist, constitute, contain, dependent, design, dissect, dominate, encompass, exclude, framework, hierarchy, include, independent, layer, mainstream, matrix, mutual, organize, portion, proportion, ratio, reciprocal, section, set, subordinate, subset, subordination, supplement, taxonomy, unit*

6. **Words about ideas**—*abstract, alternative, comprehend, concept, conjecture, generate, hypothesis, hypothetical, issue, literal, metaphorical, paradox, perceive, philosophy, relative, research, resource, source, symbol, theme, thesis*

7. **Words about cause and effect**—*affect, consequence, contributing factor, effect, impact, interact, mitigating factor, respond, result, stimulate*

8. **Words about process**—*assemble, covert, emergent, facilitate, formative, formula, formulate, hamper, hinder, innovate, latent, manipulate, method, overt, process, protocol, strategy, technique*

9. **Words about amounts and degrees**—*critical, deficient, maximum, minimum, negligible, range, significance, substantial, substantive, sufficient, unsubstantial, volume*

10. **Words about time and order**—*chronological, concurrent, contemporary, current, index, initial, intermittent, interval, overlapping, previous, prior, sequence, simultaneous, subsequent, transient*

11. **Words about systems**—*aspect, attribute, core, cycle, device, establishment, feature, function, infrastructure, institution, integral, mechanism, model, orchestrate, paradigm, regulate, trigger*

12. **Words about change and stability**—*accelerate, cease, collapse, convert, decrease, deteriorate, diminish, distort, dynamic, evolve, expand, flexible,*

fluctuate, increase, maintain, modify, pivot, plateau, radical, regener-
ate, restructure, reverse, revert, revise, revolve, rotate, stable, sustain,
transform, uniform

We believe that these words need special care and attention. Although they are at the center of academics, they often get overlooked as targets of direct instruction. Students simply don't know these words as well as we assume that they do. To close that gap, we need to:

1. Raise our awareness of these words and others like them.
2. Use these words deliberately in our classroom speech, self-translating as we do so.
3. Include these words in our explicit vocabulary instruction

As you peruse the list, you might wonder why certain other commonly used words in academic language are not present. The answer is that this is not a definitive list—primarily because there is no such thing. A definitive list would be determined by the context that your students happen to find them-selves in—a constantly moving target. Therefore, we've tried to make the list as generic and interdisciplinary as possible so as not to turn it into another subject area glossary. We think that if you raise your awareness of words such as these in your communication with students, you'll naturally bring in other words that will also serve to elevate your students' vocabulary.

Because to know a word is to be able to manipulate it into various forms, we've included in Appendix A a brief morphology (an array of word forms). Your students already know many of these forms. And to make things simple, we have chosen to include only the most common forms of each word.

You'll note that the list has a range of sophistication. Many of the words may already be known—perhaps used—by many of your students; others are elevated terms such as *paradox, inductive reasoning, proximity*. You should not dismiss generic academic vocabulary (GAV) words too hastily because you think that they are already known by your students. You should consider two factors when evaluating these words:

1. *The same word in English can have several meanings.* For example, **rela-tive** as a noun is a word that can refer to a member of one's family. Most students from middle school on probably know this meaning. However, it is commonly used as an adjective in academic discourse with a very different meaning. Imagine a student who reads about someone who is living "in relative isolation." That student may well think that the person is separated from her family! Thus it appears on the GAV even though it is a commonly known word.

2. *A word can have derivations that are unfamiliar to students.* For example, everyone in your class might know the meaning of *theme*, but many may not be familiar with *thematic*. Or, from the other direction, they probably know *constitution*, but when they encounter its base word (*constitute*), they might not make the connection.

Finally, you'll note that neither the list nor its organization into categories is set in stone. You'll find a lot of overlap. Feel free to disagree with our placement of a word into this category or that. We feel strongly, however, that words need to be clustered based on meaning, rather than just listed alphabetically.

Frequency of Occurrence

A concept all too often ignored in vocabulary texts is **frequency of occurrence**, that is, how often a given word appears in written English texts. Doesn't it make sense that we should select for study those words that are most likely to show up in the texts that our students read? Fortunately for us teachers, a lot of the groundwork has already been done. All we have to do is take advantage of it. Appendix H discusses frequency of occurrence, shows how the GAV breaks down according to frequency of occurrence, and shows you an easy way to determine the frequency of occurrence of words in any reading selection that you can submit electronically to a website.

⬤LASSROOM APPLICATIONS

Implicit Instruction

We need to make our students more familiar with academic language by (a) being aware of the words on the GAV, and then (b) using the words frequently, self-translating as we speak. It would be great if every teacher in the school had a copy of the GAV that they kept within easy reach. Kept inside a drawer, the GAV won't do anyone much good.

Remember that word-knowing is not an all-or-nothing matter: The more repeated, meaningful exposure your students have to academic language, the deeper they will get into understanding the words and, eventually, the more they will be using them to communicate.

Think for a moment about how toddlers learn new words. As caregivers, we don't think about what our target words for the day are with our little ones. We don't say, "Hmmm, today I think it's time for little Amanda to add the word 'juice' to her vocabulary." We don't even think about the words she is learning—we just immerse her in purposeful language. We hold out a container and say:

"Are you thirsty? Would you like some juice? Here, let me pour it into this cup for you? Can you hold that yourself? Careful not to spill it!" Next thing we know, there's Amanda pointing to a container (of something else, could be cooking oil) and calling it "juice." She has attained the concept of liquid in a container in the kitchen, having something to do with food. But she has learned the concept imperfectly. We don't worry that she will never understand the difference between juice, milk, and cooking oil. We assume that with enough exposure, she'll narrow her definition of juice, and someday even be able to discern orange juice from pineapple-mango juice.

Something else has happened in Amanda's "vocabulary lesson": She's learned the target word (*juice*) in conjunction with other words that tend to go with it: *thirsty, pour, cup, spill.* And that's just the beginning of a conversation about juice, a conversation that will include not only words but gestures, facial expression, vocal inflection.

Effective teachers (of any subject) develop the habit of using elevated language that they make accessible to students by self-translating and simplifying as they go. They also do that process in reverse: translating the student's "everyday" language into "academic" language. They mirror the student's words back, but they upgrade the words.

Implicit instruction on the GAV means that teachers need to use every opportunity to provide a language-rich environment that integrates reading, writing, listening, and conversation with subject area learning.

Explicit Instruction

What follows are four thought-provoking activities that deepen understandings of any grouping of words. These activities work well for the GAV because students come to this list having *some* knowledge of *some* of the words. We want to extend their prior knowledge of the words that were already somewhat familiar. Remember that word knowledge is not an "all or nothing" thing: There are intermediary steps between never having heard of a word and knowing fully how to use it. Along the way, students need exposure and engagement with new or partially known words to achieve durable learning.

You may expose the students to the GAV one set at a time, spending a week or two on each set, depending on the needs of your students. Or, you may give them the entire list, divide the students into groups and have the groups choose a set on which to work, employing one or more of these activities.

You may be fortunate enough to work in an enlightened school where the GAV is in place over a span of grade levels or across subject areas if you work on an interdisciplinary team. If that is the case, you and your colleagues will probably want to divide the words among yourselves for explicit instruction, realizing that implicit instruction needs to take place continuously.

Classify

The ability to classify is an important mental skill. The GAV is already classified into twelve subsets. However, the words within each subset may be further classified into smaller units based on meaning. The activity is to have students divide the list into at least two categories. They should give each category a name. Because the purpose of this activity is to spend time with the words to get to know them better, the forming of categories is the vehicle for learning the words, not the goal itself. Therefore, it's fine to have outlying words, words that don't fit into the categories.

Have students take the extra step of explaining and displaying their categories for the class. This allows for further meaningful engagement through listening and speaking.

Build

A word is useful only when understood in a truly meaningful context. Yet, when we ask students to "use the word in a sentence" we are often disappointed because the sentence does not clearly illustrate the meaning of the word or its natural use. In this activity, we scaffold a multistep process to build a meaningful sentence.

> **Step One:** Instruct students to create a phrase with the target word. *(Define a phrase as a word cluster that is not a sentence.) They can change the form of the word to build a phrase.*
>
> **Step Two:** Build a simple sentence from the phrase. *(Define a simple sentence as a statement that can be declared to be either true or false.)*
>
> **Step Three:** Using one of the following words (which happen to be subordinating conjunctions), build your simple sentence into a complex sentence. *The "complex-sentence-building words" (common subordinating conjunctions) are:*
> *although, as, because, if, unless*
> The value of these five words is that they are capable of creating sophisticated relationships between complete thoughts. When we teach students to use subordinating conjunctions to write sentences with new vocabulary, we make simultaneous use of instructional time, integrating a vocabulary lesson and a grammar lesson. When the sentence that they create expresses an idea related to content, we score a triple play: vocabulary, grammar, content.

Analyze

Conveniently enough, the kinds of words that we see on the GAV generally have a Latin and/or Greek etymology. That means, these words have components—prefixes, combining forms, roots, connectives, suffixes. The ability to recognize word components is an essential skill for unpacking elevated words in English. Ask students to break the words down by prefixes, combining forms, roots, connectives, and suffixes.

Prefixes

The prefix comes, of course, at the beginning of a word, changing the word's meaning. A true prefix (unlike a combining form, which we'll talk about next) can be lopped off or stuck on to the whole base word. Some prefixes, such as *non-, pre-, dis-, un-, mis-,* and *re-* are usually learned in the elementary grades. These prefixes are not only common, but they are also consistent in meaning. Other prefixes, such as *a-, de-, ex-,* and *in-* are more wily. The prefix *in-,* for example, can mean *not* (*inconvenient, involuntary*), but *–in* can also be a combining form meaning *into* (*interrupt, infuse*).

> The following poem is a playful examination of the irregularities of English prefixes/combining forms:
>
> I know a little man both ept and ert
> An intro-? An extro-? No, just a vert.
> Sheveled and couth and kempt,
>   pecunious, ane,
> His image trudes upon the captive brain.
>
> When life turns sipid and the mind is traught,
> The spirit soars as I would sist it ought.
> Chalantly then, like any gainly goof,
> My digent self is sertive, choate, and loof.

Combining Forms

A combining form is similar to a prefix in that it appears at the beginning of a word. However, the combining form is intrinsic to the word: Unlike a prefix, a combining form cannot be removed from the base word. The following words begin with combining forms: *transparent, combine, determined, export.* When used as a prefix, *ex-* means "former," as in *ex-husband.* But when used as a combining form, *ex-* means "out," as in *export.*

Some prefixes and some combining forms are called chameleon prefixes or combining forms because they change their spellings—their physical forms—to suit the word. For example, for the prefix or combining form (because it can serve as both) *sub-,* meaning "under," we have *submarine, subway, support, supplement, suffuse, surface.* Another chameleon is *co-,* a prefix or combining form that we often see as *co-, con-, com-, col-.*

So that you and your students can talk about word components and know what each other is talking about, you might want to take time to have students get their grounding on the difference between whether a word component is a prefix or a combining form. You can use the GAV, or, if you prefer, a sampling of authentic text. Make two columns: one for words having prefixes and one for words beginning with combining forms.

Roots

Next we come to roots, which are internal components bearing the core meaning of the word. (See Appendix B for an extensive list.) Latin roots are verbs. For example, the root *scribere* means "to write" in Latin. From this verb, we get all kinds words in English: *describe, description* (note how the *B* of describe morphs into the *P* of description), *scribble, prescription, manuscript,* etc. When unpacking an English word that has a Latin root, we reverse the root and the prefix. Thus, we would explain the etymological meaning of "export" as "carry out of" not "out of carry." We think this reversal needs to be explicitly taught and practiced. (For a readable and simplified explanation of why English is the way it is, we suggest a little book called *English Isn't Crazy! The Elements of Our Language and How to Teach Them* [2000] by Diana Hanbury King, York Press.)

Suffixes

Suffixes perform a different service to a word: Rather than changing the meaning of the word, the suffix changes how the word can fit into a sentence grammatically. Nouns, verbs, adjectives, and adverbs each tend to favor particular suffixes. Students should get used to trying on different suffixes to the target word. We'll say more about this when we talk about morphology.

Connectives

Finally, we have the connectives. Connectives are syllables stuck between the combining form or root and the suffix that allow the word to be easily pronounceable in English. Not all words use a connective. There are four Latin connectives: *i* (most common); *u, ul,* and *ol.* For example, in the word *addition*, *i* is the connective; in the word *subtraction*, there is no connective. In the word *speculate*, *ul* is the connective. It's useful to know about connectives because (a) knowing about the four connectives helps students see spelling patterns and patterns are an extremely powerful means of learning and (b) knowing about connectives allows us to account for all of the parts of a long word.

Two Activities

Here are two activities to help students understand the words on the GAV through analysis:

1. Have students group words according to their structural similarities: words with prefixes, words with combining forms, etc.
2. Have students create "word component kits"; these would be any kind of set of sturdy movable parts (such as large dice, strips of cardstock

paper or index cards). Students write various prefixes, combining forms, roots, and suffixes on the parts and then create words out of them. Color-code the parts. Have a device, such as small Post-it notes, to indicate spelling changes that might be necessary for adding suffixes.

Discern

Many of the words on the GAV have overlapping meanings. The ability to find differences between items that are seemingly the same is a critical thinking skill that, in itself, calls for precise language. As a way of understanding the words more deeply, work with students on clarifying the difference between the following word pairs from Set I: (*Warning:* For some of these word pairs, there may seem to be no discernible difference; however, there will always be contexts that favor one over the other. Using the second pair, below, as an example, we would never say that a property is evaluated before it is put on the market—we would say that it is assessed.)

> *analyze* and *explain*
> *assess* and *evaluate*
> *identify* and *stipulate*
> *implement* and *apply*
> *concise* and *precise*
> *persuade* and *convince*
> *well-developed* and *well-organized*
> *well-developed* and *thorough*
> *describe* and *discuss*
> *overview* and *summary*
> *review* and *critique*

Changing the Form

An important part of knowing all about a word is knowing how it changes by adding suffixes that allow it to fit into sentences. You'll see the various derivations of the words on the GAV in Appendix A. We call the collection of derivations for a particular word a *word family*. (We're clarifying the way we're using the term *word family* because this term is also used to refer to words having similar sound patterns, but not necessarily similar meanings—for example, *hat, cat, sat*. In this book, the term *word family* refers to the ways in which a single word changes to fit its grammatical context. The array of these changes is also called morphology.)

Conclusion

We covered a lot of material in this chapter—concepts and activities that will be revisited in subsequent chapters. Two main points stand out—points that bear repeating:

1. We need to make informed decisions about what words to teach explicitly. Selecting words that are too easy—words that most students already know—is, obviously, of limited value. Relying upon words that might pop up occasionally in texts or literature swings the pendulum in the other direction: Words drawn from literature, though intriguing, are often not those that the student is likely to encounter again soon. This is especially true for pre-twentieth century literature. There is a sizable body of words in between these two extremes, however, that should be the focus of your explicit instructional efforts. These are the words that teachers, textbooks, and literary works use frequently—words that will show up again and again as students progress through school. Knowing these words and their derivatives is, therefore, very valuable. We have provided you with a list of words, organized by general meaning, that is drawn from the heart of this target area: the Generic Academic Vocabulary.

2. If you want your students to truly acquire the words you target, that is, if you want them to become a permanent part of their existing vocabulary, you have to provide frequent, *meaningful* exposures to them. Use them when you teach; have students discuss how they interrelate; let students manipulate them by adding prefixes and suffixes to them or by discussing how closely related words differ.

We devote a considerable portion of the remaining chapters to ways to provide effective elaboration in the classroom. Without it, students will be superficially acquainted with the words until the vocabulary quiz; most of the words will then quickly fade.

Receptive vs. Productive Vocabulary

Definitions

As the previous chapters demonstrate, before you are able to use a word correctly and fully, you have to know quite a bit about it. An important distinction exists, therefore, concerning the words that you have locked in your brain. To capture this distinction, we use the terms **receptive** and **productive**:

- You are in **receptive** control of the words that you understand when you hear them or read them.
- You are in **productive** control of the words that you use to express yourself, in speech or in writing.

If you've ever been around toddlers, you've noticed that they *understand* words and phrases way before they can *say* them: A fourteen-month-old child, for example, may respond to language like "Let's put on our shoes. It's time to go now" well before she is able to say things like this herself. Just as this child's receptive vocabulary is

Have you studied a foreign language? If so, are you better at reading or speaking it?

People who have taken, let's say, a Spanish course or two, will normally tell you that they can read it a bit, but that they cannot speak it. If they have spent some time in a Spanish-speaking country, they will say they can read and understand the language better than they can speak or write it.

This is, of course, to be expected: it is *much* easier to be in **receptive** control of a language than to be in **productive** control.

much larger than her productive vocabulary, our students' **receptive** vocabulary remains considerably larger than their **productive** vocabulary. In fact, virtually every literate adult has a much larger **receptive** vocabulary—including, of course, you. You know lots of words that, for a variety of reasons, you simply do not use when you speak or write.

This difference in vocabularies is easy to understand. When you read or listen, the words have already been used in context; your primary job is to extract meaning from them. You are not required to know everything about a word in order to understand it fully.

Knowing a word is a matter of degrees of depth: knowing the gist of a word is, quite often, all you need when you hear or read a word. As you become better acquainted with a word, you begin to know its nuances, connotations, etc. In other words, you must be in control of a lot of information about a word before you are able to *use* it properly. Examples:

1. I (John) never use the word *aplomb*—I am not sure how to pronounce it. I also never use *comprise* because I can never seem to remember how sentences hang together with that word as the main verb. But if I see either word in a passage or if someone says either word to me, I'm fine.

2. Here are two nonsense words: *balderate* and *mamiber*. Let's imagine that all you know about these two words is that they have something to do with **killing**. If this is all you know about these words, you would not be able to use them properly in your own sentences. However, would you be able to understand sentences in which the words were used? See what you think:
   a. Pierre Gemayel was *balderated* in 2006.
   b. The soldiers *mamibered* hundreds of men, women, and children. You have enough information to be in **receptive control** of these two "words," so you are able to understand the above sentences. If we give you the actual words (**assassinate** and **massacre**, respectively), you are able to tap into the fully specified information that you possess as a native speaker and use them correctly in sentences. In other words, you are now in **productive control** of these words.

As we stated earlier, acquiring productive control over words is normally a gradual process. Bits and pieces are added to your body of knowledge about a new word as you are exposed to it in a variety of contexts and situations. Figure 4.1 provides a graphic representation of this process.

FIGURE 4.1. Receptive to Productive Control Process

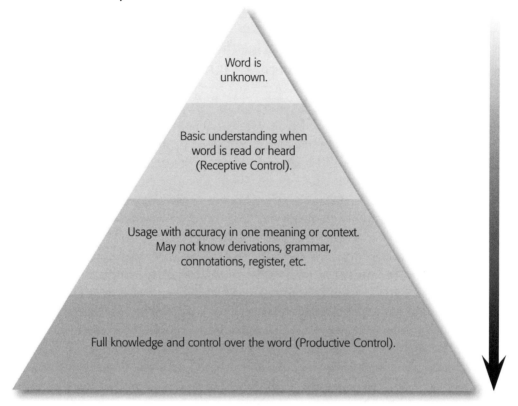

Let's take "egregious" as an example. Let's say that you see it for the very first time in the following sentence:

Deciding to ride out the storm turned out to be an egregious error.

You think that it must mean "very bad" from context, but you decide to look it up.

♦ Your definition turns out to be pretty close: the dictionary defines it as conspicuously bad. You have now moved from the first step to the second step in the acquisition process.
♦ After you see it for a couple of more times, you now feel confident using it in conjunction with "error"—the third step.
♦ However, you do not know what else can be "egregious": A house? A statement? A misrepresentation? You are not sure. You also do not know whether there is a negative (*unegregious*? *inegregious*?) or a noun

form (*egregiousness? egregiousment?*). You will need a lot more exposure to this word before you are in total productive control of it (the final step).

We will return to this whole concept later in this chapter.

●CLASSROOM APPLICATION

Students already know intuitively about the difference between their receptive and productive vocabularies. However, they have probably never thought of their relationship to language in these terms. The purpose of the following learning activity is to enhance student awareness about receptive and productive vocabulary so that they can begin to deliberately promote some of the words that they *know* receptively into what they actually *use* productively.

The teacher might give a list of some words that students are likely to identify as being in their receptive, but not their productive, vocabulary. Let's take the words in Set 1 of the list of Generic Academic Vocabulary:

analyze	critique	explain	review
annotate	debate	extrapolate	specify
apply	describe	export	stipulate
assert	determine	identify	summary
assess	discuss	implement	support
clarify	dissuade	interpret	thorough
concept	distribute	involve	well-developed
coherent	employ	overview	well-informed
comment	espouse	percent	
concise	estimate	persuade	
convince	evaluate	refute	

Students will probably acknowledge that many of these words are familiar to them, but that, now that they are thinking about it, they do not use all of these words much in their speech or writing. The goal of this exercise is to have students elevate their productive vocabulary by consciously beginning the process of moving them from the "Receptive Only" category, which we can think of as "Partial Ownership," to the "Productive" category, which we can think of as "Full Ownership."

The collection of words in the GAV are useful for academic discourse. The list should be visited often. But that does not mean that all students must learn all of the words in lockstep. We *could* march the students through the list, set by set, but that would not be likely to result in durable learning. We grow our vocabulary by building a layered awareness about words and then using them, perhaps imperfectly at first, for **meaningful communication**. In keeping with this principle, here are the steps for this activity:

♦ Begin by explaining the difference between receptive and productive vocabulary.

♦ Ask the students to plot the words in Subset 1 on a chart like the one in Figure 4.2 (page 38). Note that there are dotted lines, not solid lines, between the columns, implying that our understanding of a word can fall somewhere between the categories.

♦ After the students have set up a visual array of the words in Subset 1 on the chart, have them focus on the words in Columns 2 and 3. These are the words that they are going to target to learn more about so that they start to move from receptive into productive control. Students should target no more than ten words at a time, favoring the ones that are the most familiar or the most interesting to them.

♦ The Vocabulary Processing Chart (Figure 4.3, page 39) is a visual organizer that allows for substantial processing: The student connects the word to prior knowledge, consults a dictionary or glossary for affirmation, makes adjustments, paraphrases, reprocesses the concept into nonverbal form, and then produces a carefully crafted sentence.

♦ Have them begin to work in pairs or trios to help each other complete the Vocabulary Processing Chart. It is perfectly fine if not everyone is working on the same words, as the variety will only generate a wider "word buzz" from the GAV. And they do not have to complete charts for every word in Columns 2 and 3. Keep in mind that the goal is to have students grow their vocabularies based on their needs and levels of readiness, not for every student to process the same words.

♦ *Educated Guess:* The first step is for students to make an educated guess as to the meaning of each of the self-selected words. Encourage students to help each other so that they can voice their thoughts, engaging listening and speaking as they formulate a written definition. Chances are they will have a core group of words in common along with other words that one partner knows better than the other. We're trying to embed natural communication in the vocabulary-learning process with as much authentic communication as possible.

♦ *Dictionary:* Only after they have written their educated guess about the definition should they consult a dictionary. (If this system works the way it should, students won't just pick up the first definition in the entry. They will scan the entire definition in the hope that their educated guess matches one of the entries.) Be sure to have them use a dictionary that is age appropriate. In the lower grades, ease of use is more important than the thoroughness of the information offered by a sophisticated dictionary.

- ◆ *Paraphrase:* Now it's time for the students to process the definition by paraphrasing it. Students should write the definition in their own words, making it comprehensible *to them.* This will mean allowing them to use their own colloquial language, abbreviations, and even slang to connect the new information to their own level of understanding.
- ◆ *Visual:* The next step in the process is to reformulate the definition into a visual—a picture or a symbol. A good suggestion is to have students google the word for images. They can (literally or digitally) paste the image into the chart, or they can draw it freehand.
- ◆ *Sentence:* Finally, we want the students to contextualize the word by using it in a sentence, but not just any sentence. A good illustrative sentence needs to have substance, so we give them a minimum number of words (we suggest twelve). It also needs to have action, so we require that it have an action verb. And, to further animate it, a good illustrative sentence needs to include a visual image. *Substance, action, imagery*: These are the criteria for composing a meaningful sentence that employs a new word.

FIGURE 4.2. Receptive vs. Productive Chart

How well do you know these words?

I've never heard of these words.	I've heard of these words, but I'm not sure what they mean.	I think I know these words, but I've never used them in speech or writing.	I know these words and have used them in my speech and writing.

FIGURE 4.3. Vocabulary Processing Chart

Vocabulary Processing Chart		Target Word: _____
My guess:	Glossary definition:	Visual: (Draw or find a picture.)
	Definition in my own words:	

Complete sentence of at least _____ words.
(Must contain an action verb and a visual image.)

What's Wrong with This Picture?

Let's talk some more about using a new word in a sentence.

Learning a new word is like getting to know a new friend. At first, your knowledge is superficial—it takes time and lots of contact in a variety of situations before you really *know* this person and can establish a close relationship. The same thing is true when you first encounter a new word.

In the traditional approach to vocabulary study, students are given a list of words, many of which are brand new to them, and told to find their definitions and then to use them in meaningful sentences. A definition is the primary requirement for **receptive** control; using the word in a sentence is the other end of the spectrum—a task that requires relatively complete **productive** control. In the previous chapter, we discussed the complex body of knowledge that is required before a person truly *knows* a word. A dictionary definition often just scratches the surface; students need exposure to a word in a variety of contexts before attempting to use the word in a sentence. It's like meeting somebody for the first time at a cocktail party, chatting with her briefly, and then being asked about her character or being asked to predict how she would react in certain situations: you simply do not know her well enough yet.

When students are asked to use words in sentences before they have enough of a grasp of the details for those words, they create weird concoctions—misfirings such as the following. We've all seen them:

♦ Happiness always accompanies with you.
♦ That was a hard math assess.
♦ After two years of dating, they decided to obtain marriage.

The natural process for acquiring a new word is to figure out some general sense of what it means—usually by some problem-solving situation—and then seeing or hearing the word used in a variety of contexts. Many of the new words will remain in one's **receptive vocabulary**. Other words will gradually seep into one's **productive vocabulary**. In the traditional approach, however, let's face it—the students forget most of the words. They simply don't "invite" the words from the "vocabulary list" into their productive vocabulary. And no wonder: if we want new words to be incorporated into the existing vocabularies of our students, we have to carefully *scaffold the instruction*. We have to expect nothing more than **receptive** knowledge at first, moving slowly into productive skills as we provide meaningful exposure to the words in a variety of contexts and modes.

What might carefully scaffolded instruction look like? For one thing, there would be purposeful repetition of the words, just as there would be in a good foreign language class. The student would be hearing the word in various contexts, used as various parts of speech, morphed into the various forms that the target word can accept. It would look like a conscious effort on the part of the teacher to transition a word from receptive knowledge to productive control of the target word. It would look like an engaging, social activity that treats vocabulary learning like the natural activity of language acquisition that it is, rather than the passive exercise of filling in blanks on a worksheet. And, as you'll see in the pages that follow, carefully scaffolded instruction about a target word takes *more than the definition* into account. It considers the "care and feeding" of the new word.

Quiz

Here are a few examples of the kinds of exercises that students are often asked to do as they learn vocabulary. Your job is to determine whether they require **receptive** or **productive** control. We'll start with an easy one:

1. Use the new word in a sentence.
    Discussion: As we stated earlier, this task requires *very* productive knowledge. Traditionally one of the *first* things students are asked to do, this undertaking should be one of the *last*. And, when students do have enough control of the new word to use it in a sentence, their directions should go beyond "use it in a sentence." As stated earlier, you are more likely to get a juicy, rather than a perfunctory, sentence if you specify that you want the sentence to have any or all of these qualities:
    a. *Substance:* The sentence should have at least twelve words.
    b. *Action:* The sentence should have an action verb.
    c. *Specificity:* The sentence should elicit a visual image.
    By structuring the directions for using a new word in a sentence in this way, you are making simultaneous use of instructional time: reinforcing writing skills while teaching vocabulary.

2. I don't believe you. You are _____ a lie.
    a. speaking   c. saying
    b. telling   d. talking

    Discussion: This task also requires productive knowledge. For whatever reason, we never say someone is *speaking, saying,* or *talking* a lie. That we *tell a lie* is what is called a **collocation** (see Chapter 3). This piece of information will already be specified for us in any receptive situation—it isn't tied in directly with the meaning of the words involved. It is through repetition, as well as explicit instruction, that students get the feel for collocations. If the repetition is there but the explicit instruction is not, then there's a good chance that students won't notice the pattern. If the explicit instruction is there but the repetition is not, then there's a good chance that students won't remember the collocation because they haven't been exposed to the pattern enough.

3. Jerry was deathly afraid _____ spiders.
    a. from   c. at
    b. of   d. with

Discussion: To select the preposition that best fits into the sentence, you have to know more about the word "afraid" than its definition: You need the productive knowledge that, in this context, we say "afraid *of*." You don't need to know that "afraid" goes with "of" in the above sentence on a receptive level because the preposition will already be supplied. But you do have to know how to insert the word in a sentence using the correct preposition if you are to use the word "afraid" *productively*.

This example illustrates what's missing when we teach single words only, without their collocations. If you look at many vocabulary lists and workbooks in common use, you'll find nothing but lists of single words to look up, as if knowing the definition of a single word enables you to actually use it productively.

4. Matching: Match the words in the left column with the best synonym in the right column.
    Discussion: This task requires receptive knowledge only. When you read or hear a word, you have to have some idea about the *meaning*—context may or may not provide clues. So matching a target word (*massacre* with *kill* in our earlier example) requires receptive control only. Yet, many popular vocabulary "programs" offer little more than matching columns to serve as assessment. Matching columns don't afford us with evidence of substantial learning, nor do they provide authentic language experience when students do them "for practice."

5. The police told the _____ of the apartment that they had to vacate.
    a. people   c. occupants
    b. inhabitants   d. renters

    Discussion: Knowing the proper context or connotation for a word is definitely a productive piece of knowledge. Any of the above words would fit logically; we just wouldn't use any of them except *occupants* in this situation.

    Here's an opportunity that does have potential for durable learning if students explain why the other three choices, all similar in meaning, would not fit the bill. (Although you might not want to assess students by having them give such an explanation, it would be a good processing activity.)

6. I _____ that beautiful necklace that you are wearing.
   a. extrapolate   c. immolate
   b. covet   d. eradicate

Discussion: This time, meaning is the sole determiner for deciding which word fits in the blank. Therefore, the task requires only *receptive* knowledge.

What a fill-in exercise like this tells us is whether or not a student knows the target word, in this case, *covet*, as opposed to three other words that are very different from it and couldn't possibly be confused with it. Not bad, as long as we realize that differentiating the word *covet* from *extrapolate, immolate,* and *eradicate* is not the same level of knowledge as differentiating it from words that are closer in meaning. But, if we were to offer choices such as *want, envy,* and *admire,* the sentence would have to be more substantial:

I _____ that beautiful necklace that you are wearing, so I might purchase one just like it. (*want*)

I _____ you for that beautiful necklace that you are wearing, and I wish I had one like it. (*envy*)

I _____ that beautiful necklace that you are wearing, and I aspire to own one like that myself someday. (*admire*)

I _____ that beautiful necklace that you are wearing, and I'm not listening to anything you are saying because I can't stop thinking about how great it would look on someone with my hair color. (*covet*)

CLASSROOM APPLICATION

A key goal for vocabulary instruction is to instill in our students enough knowledge about the targeted words to allow them to keep reading without losing their train of thought and without having to stop and look the word up. Let's return to our earlier examples of **massacre** and **assassinate** to demonstrate one way.

We decided that if the students could associate **massacre** and **assassinate** with **kill** as an initial step to acquisition, they would be able to understand text in which either of these words appeared. This grouping is what we call a **keyword group**. It contains a *keyword* that students already know (**kill**), and associates words they might not know with the *keyword*. Here are two examples of **keyword groups**:

Keywords:	**to kill**	**a beginner**
Approximates:	murder	novice
	assassinate	apprentice
	massacre	Tyro
	slaughter	neophyte
	execute	greenhorn
	exterminate	newcomer
	do in	rookie
	bump off	newbie
	slay	
	put down	
	butcher	
	put to sleep	

Let's examine this approach a bit more closely.

We are building from known information to new information, helping students make the connection. In English, the same word can function as several different parts of speech. For example, one can read a **book** (noun), **book** a criminal (verb) or participate in a **book** club (adjective). The *keyword* contains clues that let students know which usage is being expanded. If students can mentally substitute the keyword for the more complicated word that happens to appear in the reading passage, they can continue reading with adequate comprehension. This ability is our primary objective.

Later, as students become more familiar with the target words (through repeated, meaningful exposure), they will refine their understanding of them, and they will move closer to productive control in various circumstances. This is to say, close enough for now is close enough for now; with carefully scaffolded instruction that includes repeated, meaningful exposure, the full meaning of the target word will emerge. The ability to use a word productively will develop on an as-needed basis, but we can coax that process along by our conscious awareness of our students' need to see and hear new words in the classroom environment.

Often, context will clarify the distinction between a *keyword* and a word whose meaning is similar to it. For example, the reading passage will almost always contain information that shows that only political figures are ***assassinated***. This more finely tuned distinction is added—slowly or quickly as the need dictates—in subsequent exposures with scaffolded instruction.

Such an approach, properly structured to minimize the rote memorization load, allows students to acquire receptive vocabulary much more quickly and efficiently than they would if we were to spend time on the specifics of each and every word. Productive control of words can—no, must—be built across time, nursed along by multiple exposures. Students need receptive control in order to understand a reading passage; building a sense of approximate meaning is an efficient way to give them exactly that.

The Keyword Map

Crovitz and Miller (2008, p. 51) devised a graphic organizer that will help students begin to get a better feel for the members of a keyword group. They encourage students to plot the approximate words along the *x* and *y* axes. Here is how the process works, using our keyword group *to kill* as an example.

Prepare a blank Keyword Map form with the keyword in the middle. Then work with students to fill in the words in the positions they feel are best. The horizontal (*x*) axis plots whether the word is used in more formal or informal situations. The vertical (*y*) axis plots whether the word is positively or negatively charged. There is, of course, no single correct answer; instead, students will debate where and how certain words are used. Three possibilities exist in the classroom that will guide the discussion for each word:

1. *Everybody knows the word.* For example, **murder** is probably a word that the entire class will know, so everyone can participate in the placement discussion.
2. *Only a few students know the word.* These students will lead the discussion, providing examples and contexts to support their position(s). Thus the students who do not know the word will hear it discussed in a *meaningful exchange*—without you, the teacher, having to come up with examples. It doesn't get much better than that!
3. *Nobody knows the word.* Now you have to take charge—not by placing the word on the grid for the students, but by providing contexts and leading the discussion to determine a final "resting place."

On the next page, Figure 4.4 shows what a blank Keyword Map might look like and Figure 4.5 shows what a completed Keyword Map for *to kill* might look like.

You might not agree with our placement of all of the keyword group members, but that is part of the beauty of the activity: there is no single right answer. Any attempt to pigeonhole language into predefined categories is going to leak. And that's exactly what generates a discussion that will help students learn, remember, and use new vocabulary.

FIGURE 4.4. Blank Keyword Map

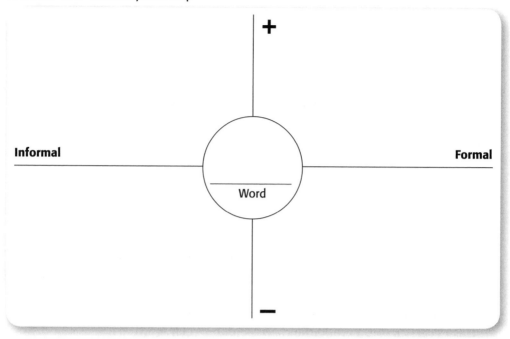

FIGURE 4.5. Completed Keyword Map

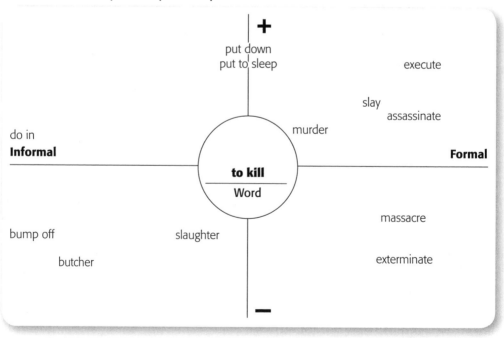

Conclusion

What can we learn from this chapter's discussion that should guide us as we plan explicit vocabulary instruction?

- ◆ Knowing how to use words when we write or speak requires control over a lot of information (see Chapter 1 for details).
- ◆ When students first study new words, their knowledge of those words is minimal; they know a rigid kind of meaning and, perhaps, they have seen them used in a context or two.
- ◆ For a word to move from **receptive** to **productive** control, students require repeated, meaningful exposure in a variety of contexts.
- ◆ Students do not need to acquire **productive** control over all of the words that they encounter. **Receptive** control is enough to allow them to continue reading (or listening) with understanding.

Brain-Based Vocabulary Learning

Natural Learning

A primary reason why we humans are at the top of the food chain is that our brains have evolved to be able to organize experiences into patterns and *learn* from these patterns. The type of learning that goes on every day in our brains is what is often referred to as **natural learning**. Let's explore natural learning to see how it might inform our vocabulary teaching efforts.

Nonpermanent Natural Learning

If we asked you to stop reading right now and list, in order, everything that happened to you from the moment you got out of bed this morning until now—would you be able to do it? Of course you could, with minimal effort and remarkable accuracy. Let's examine this ability more closely:

- When you went to bed last night, did you know *exactly* what was going to happen to you today?
- Were you born with this information?
- Did you, at some time(s) during the day, think to yourself, "I'm going to read my vocabulary book later, and those goofy authors just might ask me to recount exactly what happened to me since I got out of bed, so I had better rehearse it"?

The obvious answer to all three questions is "No—absolutely not!" So let's review: You didn't know last night exactly what was going to happen to you today, you were not born with this information, and you did not rehearse it during the day. Nevertheless, you can list these events from memory. How is that possible? You *learned* it—**naturally**. This is but one of the many things that you *learned* today without exerting any conscious mental effort whatsoever. Because the details of today's events are probably unimportant, you will soon forget them; however, at this point in time, you have pretty good recall for today's activities. So we will call this type of learning **nonpermanent**.

Permanent Natural Learning

Over the course of your life, you have learned *vast amounts* of information that are a more-or-less a permanent part of your memory. Let's explore a couple of examples.

Example #1

I. Choose the best word from the following list for each of the five sentences that follow:

a. jack   b. rich   c. foot   d. black   e. rest

1. The entrepreneur tried to come up with a
    get- _____ quick scheme.
2. When the power failed, the room became pitch _____.
3. Plug the phone into the phone _____.
4. After closing arguments, the prosecuting attorney said,
    "I _____my case."
5. This marketing campaign is very costly. Who is going to
    _____the bill?

II. Now answer the following questions:
  ♦ What other color can be "pitch"?
  ♦ Is there any other part of the body that can be used with "the bill" other than "foot"?
  ♦ How many other kinds of "jacks" can you name?
  ♦ Why don't we say, "Plug the phone into the phone hole"?
     Or "phone receptacle"? Or "phone outlet"? Or "phone opening"? Or . . .
  ♦ Is there any other word that you could substitute for "rich" in the phrase "get-*rich* quick scheme"?
  ♦ Is there any other word that you could substitute for "rest" that a lawyer might use in the phrase "rest my case" without changing the meaning?
  ♦ Is there anything else that you can "rest" besides a case where "rest" retains the same meaning?

These are just a handful of examples from the thousands and thousands of **collocations**—words that go together to form a phrase—that you know in English. When did you learn all of this? Did you study in school, for example, that you can have a "salad fork" or a "dessert spoon," but that there is no such thing as a "steak fork"? (Steak knife—sure, but not a steak fork.)

Collocations represent just one of many, many areas of **natural learning** that have occurred without any conscious effort on your part. You acquired this vast body of information because you were exposed to it over and over, in reading, in conversation, in movies and on TV (Why do we say "in movies" but "on TV"? What's wrong with "on movies" and "in TV"? When did you learn to say it this way? We could go on and on. . . .)—in short, in a wide variety of *meaningful* exchanges. In other words, your brain created the necessary network of connections through richly contextualized exposure.

Example #2
We know so many **collocations** in English that puzzles have been created based on them. As you work one of these puzzles, think about when and how you learned the necessary information:

Directions: Each answer consists of two words. Look at the clue to solve #1. The second word of the answer to #1 is the first word of the answer to #2, and so on. The answers are found at the end of the exercise.

Clues:
1. ancestry map
2. commercial forest
3. cow, sheep, or goat
4. John Belushi movie
5. feline pet
6. feline sustenance
7. nutritional guide

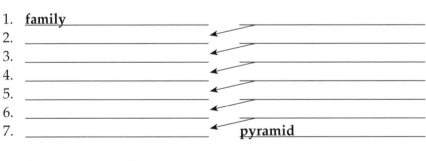

1. **family**
2.
3.
4.
5.
6.
7.   **pyramid**

Answers to exercise:
1. tree   2. farm   3. animal   4. house   5. cat   6. food

The knowledge that you possess that enabled you to solve the puzzle (or to agree with the answers when you read them) is but a miniscule sample of the vast amount of knowledge that you learned naturally as you acquired English.

Natural vs. Rote Learning

We don't need to spend time explaining and exemplifying rote learning—we are all too familiar with it. Instead, let's briefly examine how the brain forms memories and then contrast the footprint that rote learning leaves on the brain with the footprint left by natural learning. This comparison will shed light on effective versus ineffective techniques in explicit vocabulary instruction.

The Learning Brain

The brain learns by forming vast, intricate networks of connections. While we certainly are not trying to make neurosurgeons out of teachers, a basic idea about how the brain captures information serves as a nice backdrop for things to *do* and things to *don't* in vocabulary instruction.

The brain learns by forming **synapses**, connections between brain cells—and the numbers of these cells and their synapses are staggering. Your brain contains some one hundred billion brain cells—five times as many as a monkey and twenty times as many as a mouse. Each brain cell is capable of connecting with hundreds, if not thousands of other neurons. "When linked together, the number of connections our brain cells can make is estimated to be from one hundred trillion to as much as ten followed by millions of zeroes . . ." (Jensen, 2000, p. 11). As we learn, synapses are made. They are strengthened by repetition and expanded into networks by varying the input. As these new networks grow, they are further interrelated into existing networks when possible, creating stronger linkages and increasing the pathways to the knowledge.

When the brain is engaged in rote learning, relatively few neurons are involved. They fire over and over, creating a very weak set of connections that, without lots of rehearsal, fades away in a couple of days. To make matters worse, *access* to rotely learned information is very limited—you can only get to this material via the single path that was established by the rote learning process. Thus the footprint that rote learning makes on the brain is tiny. Traditional vocabulary instruction is the poster child for exactly this type of mental activity.

Picture a typical "vocabulary book." It has a list of words arranged alphabetically. Next to each word is a dictionary definition. The words are unrelated to each other and irrelevant to the student's immediate communication needs. The student is given various fill-in exercises with right-or-wrong answers. On

Friday, there will be a test in which the student will need to fill in blanks. This approach encourages—no, forces—rote memorization of meaningless, disconnected, decontextualized words. They will be there for the test on Friday, but most of them will fade into a black hole in a couple of weeks.

Let's imagine that you are a student named Emily who is tasked with learning a new word: *polysemy*.

+ On Monday, Emily looks the word up in a dictionary and finds the following definition: *having multiple meanings*. She writes down the word on one side of a flash card and the definition on the other and she rehearses the meaning.

This is where traditional vocabulary instruction stops. On Friday, Emily is asked to use *polysemy* in a sentence, which she does: "Polysemy is having multiple meanings." A week or two later, this weak connection has faded, and she has "forgotten" what polysemy means.

However, effective vocabulary instruction carries the process out much further. Let's put Emily in another kind of vocabulary class:

+ Guided by direct instruction, Emily analyzes the word and notices that it begins with a prefix that she has seen in her math class: **poly**. She remembers that in math the prefix **poly** means "many" (*polygon, polynomial*). New synapses in Emily's brain now form between existing knowledge and this new word, making it easier to recall and define.
+ Emily's teacher points out that the **sem** in *polysemy* is a part of a word that she learned two weeks ago: **semantics**. So **sem-** has to do with "meaning." Now it's really easy: **poly** = many and **sem** = meaning. Thus the word is further cemented in place by additional connections to existing knowledge.
+ Emily's teacher divides the class into small groups and asks each one to come up with words that are *polysemous*. Her group comes up with *run*; other groups suggest words like *play* and *get*. As her understanding deepens, this new word—and its derivation—is even better connected in Emily's brain.
+ A couple of days later, she is reading a really good book on vocabulary and up pops this new word! She is excited to see it and happy to know what it means without having to stop and look it up.

In the above process, you can almost feel the word take hold. The definition alone sends a single, tenuous strand of a root into the interconnected brain cells. But the continuous variety of inputs and exposures allow the root to flourish as it sends out branches that interconnect with more and more existing concepts, forming a solidly established concept of its own—naturally. The more often you are exposed to this word, the more solid the roots become. And, as the roots spread out and interrelate with other root systems, you gain more and more pathways *back* to the word—it becomes easier and easier to recall.

Now, you might be thinking, "OK, but that took a lot of class time, just to learn one word." Let's entertain that misgiving for a moment: First of all, is time better spent having Emily learn one word thoroughly and permanently, or is her time better spent learning ten words that will be dismissed right after the weekly test? Is it better for Emily to memorize ten definitions by writing them on flashcards and calling them off when prompted, or is it better for her to learn to make associations that establish new synapses in her brain? We think the answers are obvious, but we do recognize your interest in quantity as well as quality of word learning. We suggest that you use one useful word as a magnet to attract other related ones. For **polysemy**, for example, you could attract not only *semantics*, but also *semiotics*, *polygamy* (for that matter, *monogamy* and *bigamy*), which are some words related by structure. You can also attract words related by meaning, such as *multifaceted*, *adaptable*; and words related through metaphor, such as *chameleon*. Thus, we create a constellation of related words, each of which is more likely to be learned than the scattershot list of words out of nowhere.

CLASSROOM APPLICATION

To heighten students' awareness of natural learning about words, instruct them to take note of collocations that they hear and use in daily speech over the course of a day. Then have them write both words in the collocation on an index card. Let's say that you have each student hand in five collocation cards. Go through them (or have a team of students do so) to eliminate doubles. Cut the index cards in half so that each half contains a word without its partner. Post the words on the board in a random manner, forming a game board. Distribute the remaining cards. Divide the class into two teams and form two lines, like a relay race. On your signal, one student from each team has to go up to the board and match his or her card to its partner. (You can use masking tape or index cards that have an adhesive substance on the back.) Students can trade their cards in for a card in your deck, if they don't think there's a match, but doing so will cost their team some time.

The purpose of this activity is to make the point that we know a lot more about words than we realize and that words are often used together with other words in a pattern that we call collocation.

Conclusion

It makes sense to teach vocabulary in a manner that matches how the brain best learns, retains, retrieves, uses, and builds upon information. To do this, we need to help students embed new words into existing knowledge. This requires connections, connections that are strengthened through opportunities for use, repetition in a variety of contexts, recognition of words related through meaning and structure, extensions into the multiple forms (derivations), and creative applications of the word.

How Words Stay Learned

The purpose of vocabulary instruction is not for students to acquire new words for a few days. We want as many targeted words as possible to become a permanent part of their vocabulary. In other words, we are not looking to rent space in our students' brains for storage; we want to purchase it. We need to structure our direct vocabulary instruction so that the targeted words have the best possible chance of being permanently housed in our students' brains.

Having some basic understanding of how words are stored in the brain will put you in a better position to judge whether a given activity is beneficial to the storage process or not. Let's poke around inside the typical brain to see what we can discover.

Vocabulary as Entry Points to Knowledge

What if all of the information that you had stored in your brain were placed in there randomly—without any organizing principle. If you wanted to access a piece of information, you would have to begin at some random point in the pile of data and examine each piece of information until you found what you were looking for—a ridiculously slow and enormously labor-intensive process. So how *do* you find information? How are things organized so that you can access information with blinding speed and amazing accuracy and what does this organizational system have to do with the way to teach vocabulary so that it stays learned?

Let's imagine that a friend of yours wanted to know something. How would she let you know what she wanted? Words. She would probably just ask a question: *What is the capital of California? When is your birthday? What time does the party start tomorrow night?* The words would allow you to access the information she wanted in a split second. Language in general and words in specific, therefore, function as a very powerful organizing system.

To illustrate, let's list some of the information that you can tap into instantly when you hear the word "dog." You could:

- Conjure up a mental image of what a dog looks like.
- Access information about any dog you might have had as a pet—past or present.
- Imagine what a dog smells like or feels like.
- React emotionally, especially if you had had a very bad experience with one.
- Remember pleasant or funny experiences associated with dogs.
- Recall what a dog's tongue feels like when it licks you.
- Tap into a wealth of very specialized information about the animal if you were a veterinarian.
- Recall names of dogs that you or your close acquaintances had as pets.
- Know and be able to imitate the sound a dog makes.
- And so on.

It's pretty remarkable when you think about it: This single word allows you to access a wealth of information that you have placed in your brain across time from a variety of input sources—sight, sound, smell, feel, experiences, psychological reactions, schooling, etc. The word *dog*, therefore, serves as a powerful organizing principle and point of access for all of this information. Can you imagine how you could keep all of this information organized in your head if you didn't have a label?

As noted in Chapter 1, words serve as a gateway to background information that we have stored in our brains. No wonder, then, that students are unable to unlock the content of a complex reading passage if that passage has too many words that the students do not know. How can they tap into the knowledge that they already possess when they do not comprehend the entry point?

Words as Concepts

If you asked the average person on the street how words are stored in one's brain, that person would probably say that the word is connected to the thing it refers to. The previous discussion, however, indicates that the storage method is more complicated than that.

Birdiness

Think of a bird—we'll wait for you. . . .
Now answer the following questions about the bird you thought of:

1. Can it fly?
2. Can it fly backwards?
3. Does it live part of its life on water?
4. Does it live in the arctic?
5. Is it about the size of a robin?

When asked to imagine a bird, most people think of a typical robin-like bird—not an ostrich or a penguin or a duck or a hummingbird. In other words, most people imagine an animal that has all of the characteristics of a typical bird. Clearly, the word is tied closely to this central image. But is that enough to explain the storage phenomenon?

What makes something a bird?

1. It has wings. So do many insects and the occasional mammal.
2. It can fly. So can many insects and the occasional mammal.
3. It lays eggs. So do insects, fish, reptiles, and the occasional mammal.
4. It chirps or sings. So do insects and the occasional mammal.
5. It has feathers. Aha! However, if you see a chicken in the meat market that has been plucked, would you say that it should no longer be called a bird?

In point of fact, all of these characteristics need to be in place for something to meet the requirements to be considered a typical bird. Yet we allow "exceptions." An animal does not have to fly to be called a bird, for example. So, even though they are not typical, ducks, penguins, ostriches, and hummingbirds are all birds.

What We Mean by Word Concepts

Birds are not the only category of words that work in this manner. In fact, the evidence is pretty clear that everything is stored as *concepts*, as a collection of data points. When, for example, does something stop being red and start being pink? As someone begins to walk more quickly, when would you say that that person had stopped walking and was now running? When would you stop calling a structure a house, referring to it instead as a hut? In other words, every word that we have stored in our brains is a *generalization* (Vygotsky, 1962, p. 6). This generalization is formed around a concept, and the concept has characteristics.

From a space perspective, storing words as a collection of data points is a very inefficient way to keep information: we could conserve a lot of space in our brains if words could be stored in a one-to-one relationship to their referents. However, storing words as concepts allows for tremendous flexibility and creativity. Understanding words as concepts allows for much greater flexibility when we stumble upon new exemplars and experiences. It enables us to understand metaphors, an understanding that relies on our ability to see similarities in seemingly dissimilar things that, in fact, have at least one underlying concept in common. It allows us to say things like, "That looks like a bird." In other words, that thing that we see has enough characteristics in common with a bird for us to call it one. Do you, by way of further example, remember being surprised when you found out that a bat was not a bird, but a mammal? Or that a whale was not a fish, but a mammal? You were surprised because the bat shared enough characteristics with a bird to be included in your concept of what a bird is. Likewise, the characteristics of a whale fit into your concept of what a fish is.

We saw in Chapter 3 that the brain retains information by forming vast, interrelated networks of synapses. When we know a word completely, that word has tendrils that reach out into a large number of other networks, providing instantaneous access to all kinds of knowledge. When you look at vocabulary from a brain-based perspective, it makes absolutely no sense to try to teach it by memorizing words and their definitions. To do so misses out on the whole notion of learning words as concepts rather than as definitions.

● CLASSROOM APPLICATION

An effective way to build knowledge of a given word is to have students capture its characteristics through concept mapping. Concept mapping was developed by Joseph D. Novak at Cornell University in the 1960s. Professor Novak first used concept mapping as way of having students organize their emergent knowledge as they learned science. A concept map is a diagram that places the word naming the concept (e.g., science) in the center of the page. The page is then filled in with information that forms the "tendrils" that we talked about above. The "tendrils" can include:

- ◆ Kinds of . . .
- ◆ Examples/nonexamples . . .
- ◆ Required characteristics (*must haves*)
- ◆ Frequent characteristics (*might haves*)
- ◆ Associations and related ideas
- ◆ Word components

Concept maps expand the network of words that "light up" when a given word is triggered.

Concept maps should:

♦ Always be considered a work in progress because our understanding of the concept is subject to continuous change to comport with new learning
♦ Contain arrows to cross-link words from various points on the map
♦ Be asymmetrical and nonlinear

Receptive vs. Productive Revisited

When you are in receptive control of a word, you are not required to know how to pronounce it or spell it correctly. When reading, the words are already spelled for you, and you are not required to know how to pronounce them. When listening, the words are already pronounced for you, and you are not required to know how to spell them.

When you are in productive control, however, you must, at a minimum, be able to pronounce and spell the words correctly. In fact, many words remain in the receptive category for native speakers at least in part because of pronunciation or spelling. You may choose not to use a word when you write because you are not sure how it is spelled; you may choose not to use a word when you speak because you are not sure how it is pronounced. So, if you expect your students to acquire *productive control* over new vocabulary, you must include pronunciation and spelling assistance in your lesson plans.

Pronunciation

How did you learn to pronounce the thousands of words that you already know? The answer is simple: by hearing and imitating. These two channels do not change no matter how old you are. If you want your students to learn how to pronounce words, then they have to be exposed to written representations of pronunciation, they have to hear the words being spoken, and they have to be given opportunities and encouragement to use the words when they speak. In other words, giving them word lists and then letting them practice manipulating the words on paper is not enough. While formalized learning standards, such as the Common Core, may not specifically list word pronunciation as a skill, this skill is nevertheless an essential part of the scaffolding necessary to mastering the articulated speaking and listening skills.

Dictionary symbols for pronunciation, although nicely precise for those in the know, are not the most efficient way to introduce students to how new words are pronounced. We suggest using the normal alphabet. Here is an example of what we mean. Let's say that *loquacious* is a new word that you are introducing to your students. Present it as follows:

loquacious *(lo-KWAY-shuhs): talkative, wordy*

We have done three things to help students with pronunciation:

1. Divided the word into syllables.
2. Spelled the word according to how it is pronounced.
3. Capitalized the syllable that is accented.

Now, when students see new words, they can/will try to pronounce them correctly rather than assigning a best-guess pronunciation.

In the long-term, however, we encourage you to teach students how to use the symbols commonly found in dictionaries. While some Internet dictionaries have opted for the system we recommend, many either provide no pronunciation assistance or use the traditional symbols. Most printed dictionaries rely upon the traditional symbols. If students are to become independent word learners, they need to be able to reconstruct pronunciation from dictionary representations, regardless of which system they use.

●CLASSROOM APPLICATIONS

Including pronunciation cues for new vocabulary has an additional advantage for students: it helps to build fluency skills, a key component of reading comprehension. Fluency involves three skills: (a) the ability to read with sufficient speed to allow for comprehension, (b) the ability to read with a minimum of miscues (wrong words) as well as the ability to catch and correct miscues while reading, and (c) the ability to read aloud with expression.

You can see that vocabulary knowledge plays a key role in fluency. Poor readers who encounter long or strange-looking words will often not pronounce them in their heads. It is very difficult to comprehend words that we don't mentally pronounce. For one thing, we don't distinguish the unpronounceable word from a similar-looking word, resulting in lack of comprehension. For another, if we don't at least attempt a mental pronunciation for a new word, we may not recognize it when we see it again.

Thus it makes sense to not only pronounce new words for students (especially if the new words are long or strange looking), but also to have the students pronounce them. However, we don't want to embarrass students who read aloud haltingly. Nor would we have the time to hear every student read aloud. The solution is to engage occasionally in teacher-led choral reading. Even if a student "lip-synchs" while others read, there's still value in hearing the word as others read it.

Spelling

As we said earlier, a word will not become part of a student's productive vocabulary until the student knows how to spell it reasonably well. For fear of misspellings, many words don't get a chance to be up at bat simply because the would-be user is afraid to misspell them. So spelling does figure into our discussion of vocabulary growth. In some languages, such as Spanish, the spelling system coincides nicely with pronunciation. So, in Spanish, if you see a word written down, you know how to pronounce it. Conversely, if you hear a Spanish word, you know how to spell it.

Unfortunately, such is not the case with English. English borrowed words from a variety of other languages; its spelling system reflects this history. If, for example, a word came into our language from Latin, then certain spelling conventions pertain; if it came in via Greek, another set of spelling conventions pertain. For example, words that follow the "except after C" phrase in the famous "I before E" rule (receive, conceive, perceive) are Latin in heritage; words having Y as the second letter (mystery, lyric, dynamic, cycle, gyrate, hydrogen) share a Greek pedigree. People often view spelling as a hindrance to learning. However, when viewed from a vocabulary acquisition perspective, spelling is a very powerful ally. Similarities in spelling help students interrelate words into word families. For example, the words mentioned above—receive, conceive, perceive—being Latinate relatives to each other, form the nouns reception, conception, perception. Spelling clues also help students analyze new words into morphological units that can help them figure out the meaning of new words. The discovery of

> The logical absurdity of English spelling is often illustrated by the "word" **ghoti**. This word is to be pronounced as **fish**. The reasoning is as follows:
>
> ♦ Pronounce the **gh** like the **gh** in tou**gh** or rou**gh**.
> ♦ Pronounce the **o** like the **o** in w**o**men.
> ♦ Pronounce the **ti** like the **ti** in na**ti**on.
>
> *Note:* This coinage is often falsely attributed to George Bernard Shaw. See Zimmer (2008) for a discussion of its actual origin.

spelling patterns helps students create order out of chaos. When information is seen as orderly and sensible, it is easier to learn and remember.

Because going into detail about how to teach spelling is beyond the scope of this book, we will simply summarize by stating that students learn spelling from a combination of three sources of input:

1. *Spelling rules:* There are certain conventions of spelling that hold true in most instances. Properly exposing students to these conventions will help them, especially when it comes to word derivations. Examples: A *–y* at the end of a word changes to *–i* when a suffix is added (*happy* → *happily*). A word ending in a *consonant-vowel-consonant* pattern doubles the final consonant when a suffix is added (*run* → *running*).

2. *Etymology:* As previously stated, English spelling is difficult because our language has been influenced by so many other languages. Each language has certain spelling characteristics that, once learned, can make the spelling of many words more logical. We spoke a moment ago about the *cei* words that come from Latin. Words with the *ght* combination (e.g., *light, night, thought, fright, freight*) are Anglo-Saxon, and are spelled the way they are because at one time the *ght* sound was actually pronounced as the guttural sound that is heard in German, the parent language of these words.

3. *Exposure:* The primary method for learning how to spell words is to see them repeatedly in meaningful contexts. In fact, many researchers, including Stephen Krashen, believe that the best way to "teach" spelling is not through direct instruction all, but through exposure to text (2004, p. 27). According to Krashen, students and adults who read, read, read learn the patterns of spelling by way of the constant reinforcement of the visual cues on the page. Even Krashen, however, acknowledges the need for a limited amount of direct instruction in spelling to attend to certain stubborn persistent and common misspellings (2003, p. 3).

Other Considerations

Pronunciation, reasonable approximations of standard spelling, and meaning are certainly the minimal prerequisites for being able to use a word productively. In Chapter 1, we explored other areas of knowledge that you possess when you "know" a word. Figure 6.1 recaps those areas.

If all we teach in our explicit vocabulary is word + definition, we cannot expect students to be able to *remember* the words beyond the test, much less to

FIGURE 6.1. Areas of Knowledge

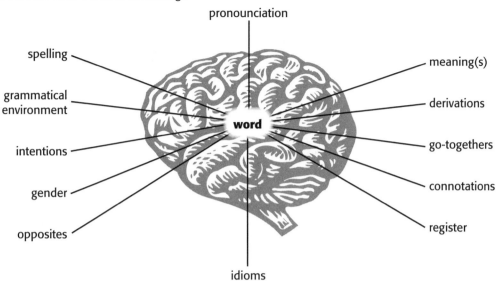

be able to *use* them effectively. William Nagy (1988) noted that three elements are necessary if we want our students to be able to retain and, eventually, incorporate new words into their productive vocabulary:

1. *Integration:* Students must be given the opportunity to incorporate new words into their existing storehouse of knowledge. You are not trying to add new words to a student's vocabulary; you are helping them to integrate new concepts into the vast network of concepts that are already in place. You are enabling your students to build networks, to interconnect an array of data points, to expand schemata.

2. *Repetition:* This word is somewhat deceiving. Nagy is not referring to repeatedly rehearsing the same information—the hallmark of rote word + definition teaching. He states that students must be exposed to new words repeatedly, in different modalities (speaking, reading, listening) and in a variety of contexts.

3. *Meaningful use:* Flash cards and word lists may be suitable as an introductory step. However, for students to truly master a word, they must be exposed to it and required to use it in meaningful situations. Incorporate new words into your teacher talk whenever possible; point them out when they appear in texts; provide opportunities for students to experiment with the words in a wide variety of situations. Keep the generic academic vocabulary list handy and draw from it often.

Vocabulary can be taught effectively only by combining these three elements.

⬤LASSROOM APPLICATIONS

Any activity that challenges students to interact with new words creatively, from new perspectives, will meet all three of Nagy's (and our) requirements. Here are some suggestions.

Think-Pair-Share

Think-pair-share is a widely used cooperative learning model in which students are given a quiet moment to think by themselves about a question. (It's usually a good idea to ask them to jot down notes.) They then exchange thoughts with a partner before reporting to the class. When it comes to vocabulary processing, think-pair-share engages students in authentic communication about their new words. But if you just ask students "what the words mean," they won't be getting the full advantage. Ask students to think-pair-share about word components (*What word roots do we recognize in our list?*), connotation (*What words have a positive connotation? Negative? Neutral?*), morphology (*What endings can a given word accept to morph it into another part of speech?*), and even spelling (*What other words are spelled in a similar way, forming a pattern?*). When doing think-pair-share for vocabulary, set it up so that the class is engaging in a variety of words.

Graphic Organizers

Graphic organizers not only help students see relationships and make connections, but they also serve as memory cues. The best graphic organizers are those that offer enough latitude that everyone's graphic organizer does not end up looking the same.

Teachers sometimes ask for clarification of the difference between a graphic organizer and a worksheet. The key difference is that, first of all, a student can create his or her own graphic organizer to serve a purpose such as "showing different kinds of . . .", "showing similarities and differences between . . .", "showing the family of . . . ," etc. Another difference between a graphic organizer and a worksheet is that a graphic organizer allows a student to work through a question to varying degrees. A graphic organizer is open-ended; a worksheet calls for right-or-wrong answers. Unlike a worksheet, a graphic organizer can often be revisited and added to as the student learns more. Graphic organizers are respected in the field because they help students construct knowledge, whereas worksheets are frowned upon because they are not thinking tools and are capable only of revealing a shallow level of factual information. Moreover, graphic organizers, unlike worksheets, take advantage of existing knowledge (schemata).

Vocabulary Games, Puzzles, Wordplay

Don't overlook the value of games, puzzles, and wordplay to reinforce and even deepen vocabulary learning. Such activities provide repeated exposure, flexibility and agility of thinking about words, problem solving, communication, and—not the least important—the fun and satisfaction that comes from language play. Language play allows for the rehearsal of new words, strengthening the synapses that turn fragile knowledge (knowledge that won't be remembered and can't be used) into durable knowledge.

Many of the concepts that we've been talking about have "play" versions. *Scattergories* and *Outburst* are games in which players engage in an exuberant brainstorming session based in categorical thinking. *Password* and *Taboo* clue-givers have to winnow concepts into single words, one at a time, while clue-receivers piece together a concept that can be named with the target word (labeling a known concept, identifying synonyms and key characteristics). *Pictionary* and the old stand-by, charades, use nonverbal expressions to convey the target word or phrase. Crossword puzzles recruit all kinds of word-learning muscles: flexibility, definition, background knowledge, recognition of spelling patterns.

Maintenance

There is no point to teaching vocabulary if the words are going to fade in the students' minds as if written in disappearing ink. Having taught words, we need to keep them in the game. We do this by continuing to model the use, in various forms, of words that we've taught. This can be accomplished through our speech, our written directions, the language that we include on teacher-made tests, word walls, notes that we write on the board, language on our websites, and informal conversations that we hold with students.

We should expect students to incorporate their new words into their writing. (We should also expect the same in their speech, although that is impossible to monitor.) To facilitate that, we should be providing word banks (suggested words to be used) for writing tasks. Ten to fifteen words is plenty for a word bank. Take time to have students talk about words that they've used for the first time or in a new form (for them).

Revisiting and reviewing words will keep them alive.

Many teachers have students keep vocabulary notebooks. Vocabulary notebooks, if used as a living resource for writing, can be very useful if students refer to them to glean ideas as they write. But if the vocabulary notebook is used only to study for tests, then it is not being used to its full potential.

Conclusion

The mind has a natural organizing mechanism, a sort of filing system that stores words for retrieval. The mind can set up more than one "filing cabinet" for a given word, thus making that word available through multiple cues. We can apply this tendency of the mind to store words in multiple groupings to our vocabulary instruction by infusing meaningful repetition, expanding word association, establishing overlapping word groups, and engaging in wordplay that generates creative, original use of words.

Depth of Processing:
The Key to Durable Vocabulary Learning

In previous chapters, we talked about the ineffectiveness of rote memorization in contrast with the vastly superior effect of meaningful elaboration. Both approaches involve rehearsal; that is, your students are repeating material in an effort to retain it in memory. So we can talk about **simple repetition**, the kind that is involved with rote learning, and **elaborative repetition**, the kind that establishes connections to other bodies of information, so as to cement the knowledge, retain it much longer, and access it much more easily.

Depth of processing is a key player in helping students move from simple repetition and temporary knowledge to elaborate repetition and long-term knowledge. A task that requires deeper processes forces the brain to allocate more of its firepower to that task. So the more you can involve your students in tasks that require deeper processing, the greater the return for the time invested. Let's explore this concept of depth of processing to see how it relates directly to vocabulary instruction.

Depth of Processing Research

A groundbreaking experiment was conducted in 1975 (Craik & Tulving) that vividly demonstrated the power that depth of processing can have on retention. Subjects were randomly divided into three groups. Each group was shown the same list of forty words, but each was given a different task to accomplish with this list:

FIGURE 7.1. Depth of Processing Test Results

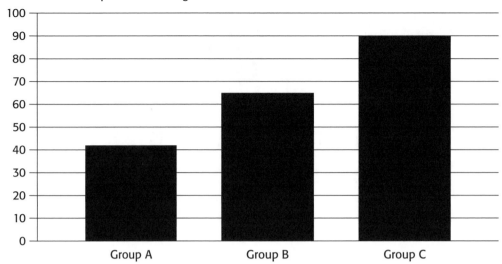

- ◆ Group A was asked to decide whether or not each word was printed in all capital letters.
- ◆ Group B was shown a word in advance and asked to decide whether each word rhymed with the given word.
- ◆ Group C was given a sentence in advance with a blank in it. Each member was asked to decide whether each word would fit in the blank.

A few minutes after a given group had completed its task, they were given a surprise test of recall: They were shown a list of 80 words, one at a time, and had to state whether or not each word was a part of the original 40 words. Figure 7.1 graphically shows the results.

This experiment speaks volumes about the power of depth of processing. As each task increased in complexity, the subjects' brains automatically allocated more resources to solving the problem:

- ◆ Group A: The task was very superficial—the subjects were not required to process the words for meaning. All they had to do was look at the surface characteristics and react: Were the words in all capital letters or not?
- ◆ Group B: In this task, the sound of a word had to be processed—certainly a deeper level than the previous group. Again, however, the group was not required to process the words for meaning. The brain's "economy of effort mandate," therefore, devoted more firepower to this task, but only enough to take care of business: Does this word rhyme with this other word or not?

♦ Group C: This group had to process each word deeply for meaning and then decide whether or not it fit in the context of the sentence prompt. For example, the subjects might be shown a sentence such as "He met a _____ on the street." Given **friend**, the subjects would press the *YES* button; given **cloud**, they would press the *NO* button. So more brain resources had to be allocated for this task: Does this word make sense in this context?

Did it take the subjects longer to perform the more complex tasks? Yes—measured in milliseconds (thousandths of a second)! Insofar as our perceptions are concerned, however, there was no discernible difference in the time taken between the three tasks. Yet the *effect* of the tasks on retention was staggering.

We do not mean to claim that, once members of Group C processed the list deeply, they would retain it better for years to come. But they certainly had a better foundation upon which to build long-term memory retention than did members of the other two groups that had processed the words only superficially, that is, on a nonmeaning basis.

Interestingly enough, another research team (Rogers, Kuipers, & Kirker, 1977) took the Craik and Tulving experiment one step further. Working with a list of adjectives, they added a fourth category: *Does the word describe **you**?* When the subjects of the experiment processed the words by relating to them personally, their recall was stronger than it was for the other three categories. The instructional implication here is that if you really want students to remember what words mean, find ways for them to relate the words to themselves. Knowing the meaning of a word may be a momentary condition, but going into a deeper level of processing—relating the word to oneself—makes it more likely that the word will be remembered.

Instructional Implications

The more *meaningful* a vocabulary activity is, the more deeply the words will be processed and the more effectively the words will be connected to other information that already resides in the brain. Word lists, flash cards, and matching exercises are examples of **activities calling for simple repetition**: repetition of a single relationship (word to definition), devoid of much meaning. Activities that require students to use or hear or read new words in a richly elaborated context (**elaborate repetition**) *automatically* call for a deeper level of processing, recruiting more of the brain's faculties, thereby creating more linkages (synapses) and enhancing recall without extra conscious effort from your students. It doesn't get much better than that!

CLASSROOM APPLICATIONS

Let's take a look at some common practices for vocabulary learning and determine whether they call for depth of processing, as opposed to superficial (easily forgettable) processing. We'll be working with a list of words drawn from *The Adventures of Tom Sawyer:*

> alabaster, clod, jeer, novice, odious, reckon,
> reluctance, switch, whitewash

Figure 7.2 lists possible classroom activities for these words. We want you to judge the depth of processing that each task would require, where 1 is the shallowest and 10 is the deepest. Write the number in the third column for each. We will then give you our take on each of the tasks.

FIGURE 7.2. Depth of Processing Exercise

#	Task	Depth of Processing
1.	Define each and write the definition.	
2.	Match the word to its definition in a matching column.	
3.	Use each word in a sentence.	
4.	Fill in the blanks in sentences having context clues.	
5.	Construct a crossword puzzle.	
6.	Solve a crossword puzzle.	
7.	Solve a word-find puzzle.	
8.	Unscramble anagrams of the words.	
9.	Draw a picture that illustrates each word.	
10.	Draw a picture that illustrates the opposite of each word.	
11.	Identify each word as one of the following: technical, generic, regional, archaic.	
12.	Complete a morphology chart for each word.	
13.	For a word having multiple meanings, select the dictionary entry that is most applicable to a given context.	

14.	Distinguish words having a positive, negative, or neutral connotation.	
15.	Choose the right word (out of a choice of two words in parentheses) in a sentence having context clues.	
16.	Make a list of synonyms for each word.	
17.	Make a list of antonyms for each word.	
18.	Act out each word in a charade.	
19.	Write a set of yes/no questions about this word.	
20.	Summarize the "whitewashing the fence" episode using at least seven of these words.	

Here is our rating for each of the tasks:

1.	Define each and write the definition.	2

This task is very superficial: students could—and probably would—zone out as they laboriously copied the definition—which might, because of its complexity, be of no value to them.

2.	Match the word to its definition in a matching column.	3–4

Although it is true that students would have to process the word for meaning, the fact that no context is provided means that very little connection is being made with existing knowledge. Therefore, the processing is relatively shallow.

3.	Use each word in a sentence.	4

As has been previously discussed, this type of traditional exercise allows students to create empty, or perhaps even incorrect usages of the target words. If you incorporate the guidelines that we recommend (see Chapter 3), then the Depth of Processing rating would jump by at least four points.

4.	Fill in the blanks in sentences having context clues.	9

An exercise such as this allows students to explore rich connections with a wide variety of previously known information.

5.	Construct a crossword puzzle.	4–5

Writing clues that would permit solvers to figure out the words allows students to explore concepts related to the meaning(s) of the words. However, the complete absence of any context does not allow for a very deep level of processing.

6.	Solve a crossword puzzle.	3–4

This task is very similar to the matching task in item #2.

7.	Solve a word-find puzzle.	1

Yuk. The only reason we didn't give this task a rating of zero is because of spelling considerations. However, insofar as helping students connect the meaning of the targeted words to existing storehouses of knowledge, this one really does not fill the bill.

8.	Unscramble anagrams of the words.	1

See #7 above.

9.	Draw a picture that illustrates each word.	9–10

This multisensory task explores a wide variety of connections, allows for a creative analysis, and helps strengthen the relationship between words and existing knowledge. However, when asking students to illustrate words, we must be sure that our directions specify that we want the drawing to be as specific as possible.

10.	Draw a picture that illustrates the opposite of each word.	9–10

See #9, above.

11.	Identify each word as one of the following: technical, generic, regional, archaic.	3

This task involves recalling peripheral knowledge about words—knowledge that might help students know when and how to use words, but knowledge that is not richly connected so as to facilitate understanding.

12.	Complete a morphology chart for each word.	5

Analyzing a word for its morphology can help connect the word to its meaning and can also help with the analysis of future words. However, the processing that is required is relatively shallow.

13.	For a word having multiple meanings, select the dictionary entry that is most applicable to a given context.	9–10

Analyzing the context of a word to determine which of several possible meanings apply is about as deep as you can get.

14.	Distinguish words having a positive, negative, or neutral connotation.	2

Students are required to have minimal comprehension of words in order to complete this task.

15.	Choose the right word (out of a choice of two words in parentheses) in a sentence having context clues.	7

Having a choice of words removes some of the deeper processing required by tasks wherein students must come up with the correct words themselves.

16.	Make a list of synonyms for each word.	6

Certainly students are required to process a word for meaning. However, the absence of any context, of any other external connection reduces the efficacy of this task.

17.	Make a list of antonyms for each word.	7

This task puts a bit of an extra twist on things by requiring students to think about words in terms of what they *aren't*, thereby facilitating deeper processing and new connections.

18.	Act out each word in a charade.	5

Students will probably try to get their teammates to say the word by one of two methods: by sound or by meaning. However, no context is supplied, so the processing remains relatively shallow.

19.	Write a set of yes/no questions about this word.	6–10

The depth of processing is directly tied to the quality of the questions that the students write. Virtually every aspect of a word can be analyzed here, from pronunciation and spelling to meaning to contexts to synonyms/antonyms, etc.

20.	Summarize the "whitewashing the fence" episode using at least seven of these words.	10

This task requires full-bore, deep-level processing. A context exists; students must look for opportunities to insert words within the retelling of an episode. Also, this task is a great example of the simultaneous use of instructional time that is needed for us to fit everything in and to integrate the language arts—literature, writing, and vocabulary.

Demonstration: Shallow Processing vs. Deep

One of the best ways to appreciate the difference between shallow processing tasks and deep ones is to try it yourself. We want you to play the role of student so that you can experience what it is like to try to learn vocabulary in the traditional manner, with shallow processing and minimal elaboration. We will then provide tasks that involve deeper levels of processing and meaningful elaboration so that you can compare the results. Appendix C contains the material and instructions for this process. If you wish to experience the power of depth of processing on your own ability to learn new words, go to Appendix C now and do the activities provided there. When you finish, return here to continue reading.

"The New" Bloom's Taxonomy and Depth of Processing[2]

One way that we can apply what we know about depth of processing in vocabulary learning is to consider the levels of Bloom's taxonomy. The original taxonomy, developed by Benjamin Bloom and his colleagues in 1956, was revised by Lorin Anderson (one of Bloom's students) in the 1990s (and published in 2001) to make it more applicable to the needs of the twenty-first century.

Figure 7.3 illustrates the difference between the Bloom's 1956 Taxonomy and the revised one by Anderson.

Note that in addition to the switch from noun to verb, the two highest levels have been changed: *Evaluating*, long considered the highest level of thinking according to Bloom, has been moved down a notch, replaced by *creating*, which is actually the new- and-improved version of *synthesis*. In other words, we are now to think of synthesis—putting things together to create something new—as being the highest level of thinking.

The taxonomy, conveniently enough, corresponds to depth of processing: The higher-order thinking skills, not surprisingly, require more depth of processing than the lower-order skills. Let's fit some learning activities for vocabulary into the House of Bloom.

On the lower end, we have *remembering*: The student can remember a given definition and give it back when asked: The student can *recognize* a definition when it appears in a matching column or multiple choice question. The student can also *supply a definition* when given the word. If this were all you wanted,

[2]http://eprentice.sdsu.edu/J03OJ/miles/Bloomtaxonomy(revised)1.htm.

FIGURE 7.3. Bloom's and Anderson's Taxonomies

Bloom, 1956	*Anderson, 2001*
Knowledge	Remembering
Comprehension	Understanding
Application	Applying
Analysis	Analyzing
Synthesis	Evaluating
Evaluation	Creating

you could use a prompting device such as flash cards to get the student to pair X with Y (word-definition). It wouldn't matter if the target word had nuances, could be used metaphorically, was related to other words with the same components, was archaic, was associated with formal or informal register, or anything else. All that would matter would be that the word prompts another word or phrase which is its designated "definition."

One step up, but still on the lower end, we have *understanding*. The student who understands the meaning of a word can manipulate or stretch its definition a bit, can *supply synonyms* for its definition, can name its opposite. The student who understands a word can give an example and a nonexample of it, can classify it, can comprehend the meaning of a sentence containing it, can use it to unlock the meaning of other words in its sentence that may not be known. The student can compare and contrast it to other concepts, draw it, explain it to others, make inferences when it is used. In other words, the student who understands the meaning of a word has much more power of thinking because of that word than the student who has merely memorized a definition, so the distinction between the first two levels on Bloom's taxonomy is an important one.

Now we come to application, in other words, implementation or execution of the word. When it comes to word learning, this is where the student would be going from receptive to productive vocabulary. (You can understand a word *receptively* and yet not be at the point where you'd use it *productively*.) So it would be at this point where the student would develop and demonstrate control of the word by using it in authentic language. Here's where "and use it in a sentence" comes in. The student can also achieve and demonstrate application of a word by drawing it, collecting images of it, telling a story that illustrates its concept, and solving or making up a puzzle with it.

FIGURE 7.4. Common Academic Polysemes

area	extreme	origin	reaction
cell	fact	plot	remainder
common	factor	power	root
complementary	function	prime	solve
cube	graphic	product	tangent
depression	imaginary	property	value
determine	mean	prove	variable
difference	multiple	radical	
digit	operation	rational	

Climbing up to the higher levels of thinking, we next have *analyzing*. Here's where the word components come in. The student can analyze the word internally, forming connections between its components (*prefix, root, suffix*) and other words having those components. Of course, the prefixes are usually limited in meaning (*pre-, re-, anti-, ante-*, the prefixes for numbers, the prefixes for negation, etc; these are obvious once you know them). Many of the suffixes simply enable the word to have the right grammatical form for its job in a given sentence (*-ing, -ed, -er, -est*, etc.). But sometimes, the suffixed word has a meaning that becomes richer when we analyze the base word: for example, we're so used to using the words *vacation* and *recreation* that we may not connect them to their base words, *vacate* and *create*. When we analyze, we get new insights. Students become more analytical about words when they plot them on morphology charts, brainstorm all the different prefixes and suffixes that a target word can have, create semantic maps. A semantic map is a kind of "family tree" for a word, revealing its relatives that have the same root. Semantic maps can also display a word's synonyms and antonyms. Differentiating is a form of analysis. When it comes to words, we differentiate words with similar meanings: What is the difference, if any, between these sets of words?

Set One: *punitive, vengeful, spiteful, strict*
Set Two: *mitigate, excuse* (verb), *relieve, justify*
Set Three: *clarify, explain, review, illuminate*
Set Four: *hate, despise, loathe, resent*
Set Five: *fickle, changeable, unstable, inconsistent*

Another form of analysis is what we do when we trace the etymology of a word to discover how its meaning changed as it wandered far and wide through time and culture. If we know, for example, that the word *docile*, which today means *nonaggressive*, originally meant *able to be taught* (related to the root *doc*, to teach, as in *doctor, indoctrinate, orthodox*), we get deeper insights into the word *and* its concept.

And a fourth way to be analytical about vocabulary is to consider words whose meaning changes from one domain to another. The language of school is filled with such words, called *polysemes*. Think, for example, how the words in Figure 7.4 are used in different subject areas of a student's day:

The graphic organizer shown in Figure 7.5 may be used to process polysemes in terms of how a given word has a variable meaning.

This graphic organizer is for polysemes of math/science, but can also be used for social studies and other subjects, as you can see from the list. As students work through this graphic organizer, they may discover connections that get them into the heart of a word. (Many teachers, in their zeal to teach a domain-specific meaning, discount the students' prior knowledge of how a

FIGURE 7.5. Math/Science Polysemes

Words with Many Meanings

Science meaning:

_____
Word

Conversational meaning:

Visual:

Math/Science sentence: _____

_____

_____

_____

_____

Conversational sentence:_____

_____

_____

_____

FIGURE 7.6. Phrasal vs. Latinate Verbs

Phrasal	Latinate
put up with	endure, tolerate
step up	intensify
throw out	discard
take back	revoke
think about	consider, contemplate
put out	extinguish

word may be used in another subject area: "You're in *math* class now!" In fact, we can romance that prior knowledge so that the students see connections, rather than divisions, between subject areas. Such connections strengthen learning, encourage synthesis, and increase the odds that the information will be retained.)

Now we'll move up to the next level of thinking, which is *evaluation*. Evaluation is closely related to comparison/contrast because in making judgments about relative value, we'd have to compare and contrast our options. Here, the evaluation would involve word choice, also known as diction.

When we write or speak, we make decisions about register, or degree of formality, for the audience and purpose. Word choice plays a key role in register. A good example of how this works vis-à-vis vocabulary is the decision that we make about using a phrasal verb or a Latinate verb. Phrasal verbs are two (or more) word verbs consisting of a short verb plus an adverb, which some grammarians call a particle. (This adverb/particle looks an awful lot like a preposition, but it is not functioning as a preposition. For example, when we say "Turn on the light," "on the light" is obviously not a prepositional phrase.) Figure 7.6 illustrates the difference between the (informal) phrasal verb and the (more formal) Latinate verb for roughly the same concept. (See Appendix E for a fuller list of phrasal verbs and their Latinate counterparts.)

To engage phrasal verbs and their Latinate counterparts in an activity that calls upon evaluative thinking, we might ask students to judge the level of formality of a given text (a movie review, a sports article, a play, a novel)—or, of the characters in that text, based on diction.

On the creative level, we might ask students to compose and enact a skit in which two people use two different registers to work out a conflict or express an opinion. Or, we might ask them to express the same message using different kinds of diction (conversational, formal, technical). These are decisions that all writers must make. They do so on the basis of what is called the "rhetorical triangle," a relationship that consists of the speaker/writer, the audience, and the purpose. These three factors determine the level of formality, and when the speaker/writer is "off," failing to meet the expectations of the audience, then the purpose may not be achieved.

Finally, we want to emphasize that depth of processing for vocabulary is not a solitary pursuit. The further up we go on Bloom's taxonomy, the more necessary—and natural—it is to have students communicating with each other about the words.

Conclusion

A single quick exposure to a word, such as memorizing a synonym or figuring it out based on how it might be used in a single context, is insufficient for durable learning. It is necessary to provide students with thoughtful processing experiences. Because we always have a limited amount of time to devote to explicit vocabulary instruction, we need to choose words for explicit instruction carefully, favoring words that are the most useful and most conducive to the learning of other related words. If we can embed a vocabulary processing experience with another writing experience (especially one about literature), then we've wisely compacted our instructional time.

Guessing from Context

Although the direct, explicit teaching of vocabulary to students at all grade levels is critical, we fail our students if we stop there. Although one of the ultimate goals is certainly to augment our students' vocabulary, another very important goal is to make them independent word learners. Independence, for the most part, is a function of two factors:

1. Instilling a *curiosity* about words
2. Developing the skill of analyzing words to figure out what they mean

Word Curiosity

A curiosity about words simply means that whenever students encounter new words (especially repeatedly), they are not content to ignore them—they want to try to figure out what they mean and, should the words appear to be potentially useful, try to incorporate them into their productive vocabulary. As students acquire a greater vocabulary, as they acquire a critical mass of known words, they encounter fewer unknown words and are increasingly willing to pause to see if they can ferret out their meanings.

As someone who has chosen teaching as a career, you undoubtedly have a highly developed curiosity about words. Your vocabulary is probably so large that you are surprised on those occasions when you encounter a brand new word: "Wow, I've never seen that word before in my life. I wonder what in the world it means?" You also have highly developed word attack skills that allow you to gain a sense of what the new vocabulary item means. Furthermore, you have vast networks of information to which to attach a new word. If you happen to encounter that new word a couple of times, you have a very good chance of absorbing it into your receptive vocabulary, making it easier to acquire new words as you come across them. Your students, however, are not there yet.

So far, we have dealt with word attack skills that are *within* the word: Prefixes, suffixes, and word roots provide good initial entry points for attempting to guess the meaning of a new word. Context—information that exists *outside* the word—is the other major source to tap when analyzing new words. These two avenues are not one-or-the-other; they work in tandem to produce informed guesses about word meaning.

Context

As word curiosity developed, you began to derive ways to figure out what words mean by looking for clues in the language and events that surrounded their usage. This skill probably came fairly easily to you; such is not always the case with everybody, however. Quite often, your students need some guidance and assistance with this task, a skill set that is not easy to teach:

- It is human nature to believe that anything that comes easily to you comes easily to everyone, so there really is no need to teach it.
- Because finding contextual clues was easy for you, you are not consciously aware of the processes involved in doing so. Remember the physics or math teacher who could solve problems effortlessly but could not teach others how to do so themselves? The situation is analogous.
- The kinds of contextual clues that are available vary widely, so they do not readily lend themselves to simple categorization.

Despite those difficulties, you *can* help struggling students improve their ability to extract clues from context.

How Many Unknown Words Are Too Many?

If a passage contains too many unknown words, especially about information that is unfamiliar to begin with, readers cannot build enough of a context to be able to mine it effectively for clues. So the question that is commonly asked is, "How many new words within a passage are too many?" Imagine a student with scant experience reading pre-twentieth century literature and who has no idea what the Hudson River Valley looks like. Reading the opening sentence of Washington Irving's *The Legend of Sleepy Hollow*:

> In the bosom of one of those spacious coves which indent the eastern shore of the Hudson, at that broad expansion of the river denominated by the ancient Dutch navigators as the Tappan Zee, and where they always prudently shortened sail, and implored the protection of St. Nicholas when they crossed, there lies a small market town of rural port, which by some is called Greensburgh, but which is more generally and properly known by the name of Tarry Town.

Now imagine how that student feels when soldiering on to the next sentence:

> This name was given, we are told, in former days, by the good housewives of the adjacent country, from the inveterate propensity of their husbands to linger about the village tavern on market days.

Let's proceed to the third sentence:

> Be that as it may, I do not vouch for the fact, but merely advert to it for the sake of being precise and authentic.

Three sentences. How many unknown or puzzling words? The sentences are not only long, but have lots of phrases set off by commas. The unknown words, and there are lots of them, are like berries way inside a thorny bush. You can see them clustered together in there, but the thorns surrounding them make them so hard to get at. Yet, that is exactly how real words appear in real literature. Embedded in ornate syntax, they may be completely unknown (*coves, advent, vouch*), or used in an unfamiliar way (*bosom, expansion, indent*), related to nautical jargon (*shortened sail*) or, oddly enough, familiar but only in a mathematical way (*denominated, adjacent*). They may be stuck together in an impenetrable knot (*inveterate propensity*). They may be the kind of words that appear frequently in literature but seldom in conversation (*implored, prudently*). They may be unfamiliar forms of known words (*spacious*). They may even be proper noun religious allusions commonly found in literature (*St. Nicholas*).

The Legend of Sleepy Hollow maintains this level of vocabulary throughout its pages. And this story is commonly anthologized in collections meant for students as young as middle school. That may raise your awareness of just how difficult the vocabulary is in some of the literature that we expect students to understand. Stories by authors such as Edgar Allan Poe, O. Henry, Nathaniel Hawthorne, and Stephen Vincent Benet are also commonly served up to students whose vocabulary skills are not nearly matched the task. Again, the vocabulary—distant as much of it is for struggling students—is buried within all kinds of detailed description, allusions, subtle irony, meandering syntax, and archaic language. What we're talking about is an extremely heavy information load that demands multiple strategies, strategies that only motivated readers would know or bother to activate.

We would certainly have to scaffold this reading experience, without trying to focus on every single word that the students might not know. They need to understand the gist (which we might have to give them), build details upon the gist (which would be the result of their reading comprehension), be able to picture the scene (actual pictures would help), and follow the story arc. To grow their vocabulary by doing this, they need to marshal the information that they *can* get from the words that they *do* know. Key questions: *What can we picture? What do we know is happening?* Once we nail that down, we can ask: *What words do we almost know?* Then: *If you could learn just one word in this paragraph that would help you understand something that you think is important, what would that word be?*

We've been looking at text that is studded with many unknown words like stars in a clear night sky. However, there are times when the number of unknown words in a passage is small, but the information load that they carry requires the reader to know them in order to understand the message. In the following passage, we have substituted nonsense words for two real words. Can you figure out what the nonsense words are from context?

Lurfing from ralonment is governed by the same system that activates your **fight-or-flight response**: the sympathetic nervous system. This system is involuntary, meaning you don't actually have to think to carry out the processes. In contrast, moving your arm is a voluntary action; you have to think about it, no matter how fleeting the thought is. This is good, because if moving your arm was involuntary, people would end up buying a lot of stuff they don't want at auctions.

When you're raloned, your body releases adrenaline. This hormone acts as a natural stimulant and has an array of effects on your body that are all part of the fight-or-flight response. Adrenaline speeds up your breathing and heart rate to prepare you to run from danger. It causes your pupils to grow bigger to allow you to take in as much visual information as possible. It slows down your digestive process so that the energy can be redirected to your muscles. All of these effects account for the jolt you feel when you find yourself raloned. (Clark, 2008)

In the above passage, **lurfing** is used once and **ralon** is used three times, once as a noun and twice as a verb. What do you think the real words are?

Now read the passage again after reading this clue: lurfing = blushing and ralon = embarrass.

Even though only two of the 176 words in this passage were unknown, the information load that they carry makes it difficult for you to get some sense of the actual concept that underlies each one. So, what we've seen is that it isn't so simple to just "use context clues" to unlock meaning. Sometimes, we need more explicit help than that bit of commonly given advice.

Dictionaries

Why not just look every new word up in a dictionary? Well, for one thing, doing so is very inefficient. Readers must interrupt the flow of information, their train of thought, to engage in the time-consuming process of finding the target word in the dictionary. If fluency is already a problem, as it is with challenging literature, then readers can't afford a break in concentration. To make matters worse, once readers find the definition, it often contains words that they do not know. Finally, they may encounter words with multiple, unrelated meanings (polysemy). Which one fits? Only context can answer that question. Take *fly* for example:

1. He caught a *fly* that was buzzing around his food.
2. The outfielder caught a *fly*.
3. He caught a *fly* in his *fly* while *fly* fishing.

In the above examples, *fly* is used in four very different ways, resolvable only by context.

Contextual Clues

In his 1999 monograph *Three Arguments Against Whole Language & Why They Are Wrong*, Stephen Krashen classifies context effects in four ways: They can be overdetermining (where there is no need to know the meaning of a given word because the context is so familiar); underdetermining (where there would be no way to figure out a given unknown word because the context clues are absent or vague); partly determining (where the reader stands a pretty good chance of making an accurate guess based on context); and, interestingly enough, deceptive (where the context would actually be misleading). This classification serves as a good reminder that, while guessing from context is a valuable skill, it is certainly not a magic bullet.

Although it is difficult to make a definitive list of ways to derive meaning from context, we can make several suggestions:

♦ Begin your guessing-from-context activities by working with unknown nouns and verbs. Research supports what common sense would tell us: nouns and verbs are easier to guess from context than are adjectives and adverbs (Na and Nation). In fact, you can often skip unknown adjectives and adverbs without losing the train of thought or the story line. You lose some of the flavoring, to be sure, but only occasionally do you miss vital information.

♦ Think in broad terms about new words at first: *Is this word good or bad? Is this a tangible thing or an abstraction, such as an idea or quality?*

♦ Accordingly, encourage students to tolerate vagueness with unknown words. As long as they get the general idea about the concept expressed by an unknown word, students will usually be able to grasp the essence of a reading selection. If subsequent reading casts doubts upon their guesses, only then do they need to rethink or look up the target word(s).

♦ Tell students not to stop reading as soon as they encounter an unknown word. Often, contextual clues come in sentences that immediately follow the new vocabulary item. Here are some things to look for, using the word *homeostasis* as an example:

- *Appositives*: If authors suspect that the readers may not be familiar with a term, they may provide a definition or further information in a noun phrase that immediately follows the term. We call such noun phrases appositives.

  > *Homeostasis, the maintenance of one's internal environment within tolerable limits, is basic to the study of physiology.*

  Because authors use appositives a lot, and because appositives are great context clues, it makes sense for us to spend time teaching students to recognize them: Look for those comma pairs and ask yourself whether you can insert the phrase "In other words" before the words that are set off by commas. If you can, then you have an appositive and an important overt context clue.

- *Restatements*: Authors may also provide defining information in the next sentence.

  > *Doctors look for signs that the patient is unable to maintain homeostasis. Seeing that the patient's body is unable to keep vital functions within certain limits is a strong indicator of disease.*

  Teach students to keep relationships from one sentence to another in mind as they read. Nurture in them the habit of linking the end of one sentence to the beginning of the next.

- *Examples*: Another way that authors relate further information about a term is by providing examples.

  The ability of the body to maintain homeostasis is critical to one's health. If one's temperature, heart beat, or blood pressure are not kept within acceptable limits, then. . . .

  Teach students that when authors want to give you an example, they don't always say "for example." Authors sometimes use colons, if . . . then statements, or lists of concrete visuals to present examples.

- *Transition words or phrases*: Contrasts, comparisons, conditions, and the like can help readers understand a term by exploring various areas involved in its meaning.

  Homeostasis is crucial to one's survival.
  On the other hand, . . . (here comes information that is in contrast—data that may help the reader understand.)
  Similarly, . . .
  If . . .

Modeling

The single most important thing you can do to help your students see how to guess words from context is to show them how *you* do it by employing multiple strategies. The process takes very little class time. Tell them that you are going to pretend to be one of them, showing them how you find clues to words that you think might be problematic for them. Then read a short passage out loud to your students, stopping to think out loud as you process information. There are three very important points to keep in mind:

1. Do not do this activity for very long. Fisher and Frey (2008) recommend frequent modeling sessions, spending no more than five to ten minutes per session (p. 48).
2. Remember that the purpose of this activity is *not* to teach specific words and *not* to teach the concepts that the text covers. The goal is to demonstrate *strategies* that you use to figure out what words mean or how you derive meaning from a text.
3. Think like a student! Be on the lookout not only for words that some students may not know, but also be on the alert for words that could be misinterpreted because they have multiple meanings.

CLASSROOM APPLICATIONS

Strategy modeling in frequent, short bursts lays an excellent foundation for students to use in follow-up activities.

1. Give students short passages with nonsense words inserted for known words. Students then work in groups to come up with best guesses of the original words. When everyone is finished, compare answers and the reasoning processes that were used.
2. Divide students into small groups and give each group a passage that contains some words that students will either not know or might be confused by.
    a. Hand out an Unknown Word Chart filled with the targeted words. (See Figure 8.1, page 88, for an example.)
    b. Groups fill in the Predicted Meaning column with their best guesses before reading the passage.
    c. They work together to derive their best guesses from the passage, putting them in the third column.
    d. In the fourth column, they can either jot down how they derived their meanings (Context Clues) or look up words in a dictionary for comparison.
    e. When everyone is finished, compare answers and the reasoning processes that were used.
    f. Have students find short passages and underline words that they think their peers will not be able to define. Exchange passages and complete an Unknown Word Chart as described above.

Try it yourself. Figure 8.1 contains six candidates, taken from a paragraph from Mark Twain's *Puddin'head Wilson* (Courier Dover Publications, 1999) that has been selected for close examination. Fill in column 2, read the paragraph, and then fill in column 3. The paragraph itself is below. You will probably miss a couple of predictions, but be able to figure things out once you read the passage.

In babyhood Tom cuffed and banged and scratched Chambers unrebuked, and Chambers early learned that between meekly bearing it and resenting it, the advantage all lay with the former policy. The few times that his persecutions had moved him beyond control and made him fight back had cost him very dear at headquarters; not at the hands of Roxy, for if she ever went beyond scolding him sharply for "forgett'n' who his young marster was," she at least never extended her punishment beyond a box on the ear. (p. 18)

FIGURE 8.1. Unknown Word Chart

Word	Predicted Meaning (No Context)	Guessed Meaning (From Context)	Context Clues or Dictionary Meaning
cuffed			
unrebuked			
meekly			
former			
persecutions			
box			

Conclusion

In informational texts, especially textbooks, authors tend to give overt context clues, especially for technical terms that they explicitly want the reader to know. But authors of literature use words in more subtle ways. The context may or may not yield sufficient information. The reader needs to call upon other strategies, such as scaffolding to get the gist, analysis of word components, thinking about possible metaphorical meanings, tolerating vagueness until a word reveals its full meaning (if it ever does), and, yes, ignoring a few unknown words while absorbing the bigger picture.

Assessment

What are the best ways to assess the extent to which students have benefited from vocabulary instruction? To answer this question, let's have a look at what we want to happen as a result of explicit vocabulary instruction.

1. **Expansion:** We want students to have more words in their vocabulary inventory and to know more about the words that may have already been there when we started.
2. **Retention:** We want students to actually keep the words that we've taught them explicitly. Forever.
3. **Use:** We want students to move words from receptive into productive control. Also, we want them to use the words flexibly, being able to change their forms, stretch their definitions, to use the words creatively and to understand them when they are used figuratively.
4. **Strategy:** We also want them to learn how to learn words.

Looked at through the lens of expansion, retention, use, and strategy, we'd say that traditional assessments are getting the job done only partially. That is to say, our assessments need to be more accurate and more comprehensive. Humans (including students!) know words on a continuum:

♦ At one end are those words about which we have very nonspecific acquaintance—we are only vaguely familiar with their meanings.
♦ At the other end are those words that we have, for whatever reason(s), completely mastered.

The remaining vocabulary items can fit anywhere along this continuum. Continuous, meaningful exposure will allow students to master words with increasing precision, moving them farther along on the continuum. It is easily possible to use assessment measures that measure knowledge from one end of the spectrum ("Use these words in sentences.") while virtually ignoring knowledge that might be further back along the continuum. It is also possible that our assessments could cause us to overlook the kind of vocabulary growth in which a student's knowledge of a word has advanced along the continuum, but has not advanced far enough to register on our assessment.

As we have said many times throughout this book, traditional vocabulary instruction has consisted primarily of word lists, definitions, rote memory, and "use it in a sentence." We are advocating integration and meaningful elaboration. So, our assessment practices must reflect this fundamental change. The tests that we give you in Appendix D over the ten words that you learn are typical vocabulary exams. What follows are examples of test items that more thoroughly and accurately measure how well you have integrated the meanings of these new words.

Receptive vs. Productive Control

Receptive Control

Because receptive control means that students have some feel for the meaning of the words, a test of receptive knowledge should not, for example, require students to use the words in sentences or to decide whether or not various usages are correct. However, if you have incorporated all three of Nagy's requirements (integration, repetition, and meaningful use—see Chapter 6) into your teaching efforts, your students will be able to respond to more meaningful kinds of test questions at the receptive level. Imagine, for example, that *dormant* was a word that you had been working with in class. Here is a question that requires a deeper level of knowledge than typical matching or fill-in-the-blank tests require:

1. Give an example of something that might be *dormant* for a period of time.

The obvious problem with this type of testing is that it takes much longer to grade than a matching or multiple choice format. Although not as elaborative, this type of testing can be done in a multiple-choice format. Here is a possible alternative for the above question:

1. During which of the following seasons is something most likely to be *dormant*?
    a. spring
    b. summer
    c. fall
    d. winter

Productive Control

At the other end of the spectrum lie tests that require productive control. The ultimate test of productive control is to use words in meaningful sentences—a task that requires almost complete mastery of the intricacies of the target vocabulary. We have two caveats to issue about this type of assessment:

1. Do not require students to use words in sentences until they have been exposed to the words several times in a variety of contexts and modalities.
2. As we have stated before, do not simply instruct students to use words in sentences. Otherwise, you might receive answers such as the following, which legitimately respond to your prompt, but provide very little indication about how much the students actually *know* about the words:
   a. We have studied the word dormant.

Instead, include very specific instructions regarding the length and content of the sentences. We suggest that when you ask students to use a word in a sentence as an assessment, you set parameters such as these:

+ The sentence needs to have substance. That is, it must be sufficiently long to supply enough context to convince you that the student knows what the word means. We suggest fifteen to twenty words, not counting any "filler" words such as "very."
+ The sentence needs to contain a visual image in it. The visual image does not necessarily have to relate directly to the target word. By asking for a visual image, we are actually making the student's job easier.
+ The sentence needs to have at least one action verb. This will animate the sentence. Of course, the target word itself might be the action verb.
+ Finally, the sentence must have a narrative structure. That is, it must convey a little story, a story having a beginning, middle, and end.

If these requirements seem overly demanding, remember that all four criteria actually work together. Also, remember that by structuring the assessment in this careful way, we are making simultaneous use of instructional time: working on sentence-building skills as well as vocabulary. This approach is in line with the Common Core's advocacy of integrating, rather than isolating, instruction across the strands of reading, writing, speaking and listening, and language.

Shallow vs. Deep

Because "knowing a word" is not an all-or-nothing thing, but has gradations of depth, in your assessment you need to ask yourself how much knowledge of the target words you are after. Just as vocabulary tasks can require a deeper or more shallow level of processing (see Chapter 6), vocabulary tests can require a deeper or more superficial amount of knowledge about the words. In the following examples, each question requires a greater depth of knowledge about the word in order to answer it successfully:

1. A **plateau** is a kind of
   a. musical instrument
   b. communication device
   c. office building
   d. geographical feature
2. A **plateau** has which of the following features?
   a. level surface
   b. mountains
   c. inclined surface
   d. drinking behavior
3. A **plateau** is about one's
   a. personality
   b. level of achievement
   c. sleeping behavior
   d. body size

About Formative and Summative Assessment

A good assessment plan includes both formative and summative assessment. Because the difference is easy to forget, we'll clarify: "Formative assessment is assessment that is meant to guide both teachers and students toward the next steps in the learning process. Formative assessment differs from summative assessment in that summative assessment has an air of finality" (Benjamin, 2008, p. 3). A typical summative assessment protocol for vocabulary would be that the students are given a weekly test on, say fifteen to twenty words taken either from literature or from a vocabulary workbook. After several such tests, there is a cumulative test that brings together about 100 words, tested in more or less the same format.

As teachers in a traditional environment, we are probably more comfortable with summative assessment than with formative. This is because we tend to equate the assessment with grades. Grades are highly judgmental "good or bad" measurements that "count." However, formative assessment does not "count" in the same way that grades do. To use a sports analogy, summative assessment is like the game; formative assessment is more like the practice.

We are suggesting that you consider replacing many of your summative assessments for vocabulary with formative assessments. Formative assessments, being more subtle than summative assessments, are capable of revealing more about the degrees to which students know words. As you read the formative assessment experiences described in the next section, keep in mind that formative assessments are not "graded." Rather, they are used as information that should guide learning and instruction.

Formative Assessment

We realize that you don't have the time to read and evaluate complex vocabulary assessments when you are devoting so much time to reading student writing. Therefore, what we're suggesting is a blend of the two: Why not have students show their knowledge of vocabulary in the context of the writing that they are doing, and you are reading, anyway?

Here's how it might go: The students are reading *The Giver* by Lois Lowry. You, with their input, have generated a vocabulary list such as the one that is given in Figure 9.1.

You are asking them to write about *The Giver* anyway, so why not have them enrich their writing with the words that are already embedded in the story? Their ability to do that would measure their productive knowledge of the words. Of course, it would be ridiculously contrived to ask them to use *all* of the words in a unified writing piece on *The Giver*. But if you asked them to use, let's say, five of the words in the course of their response to a prompt, it would mean that they would have to peruse the list *as a writing tool*, engaging in critical thinking as they select and reject words that would fit in with what they have to say. If you use a rubric, include "use of suggested vocabulary" as one of the traits.

We think that what we're suggesting here for getting students to use new words taken from literature is better than the old "use it in a sentence" assessment. We think the difference is that we're asking the student to use the word in a sentence that exists in a larger context *about the literature from which the word was taken*. In contrast, when we ask students to "use it in a sentence" without any context, students often write sentences that are meaningless and shallow. We want to see the words embedded in something that the student has to say about the literature.

FIGURE 9.1. Vocabulary from *The Giver*

ironic	jeering	palpable	apprehensive
ponder	enhance	chastise	petulantly
droning on	hovered over	reflective	hoarded
primly	infraction	prodded	relinquish
exuberant	somber	transgressions	audible
throng	steeled himself	tentative	quizzically
weary	fretful	admonition	fleeting
wryly	sinuous	exempted	assuage
tortuous	flailing	carnage	stench
obsolete			

An alternative is to have the students ask and answer a series of questions about *The Giver*, deploying the words as they do so. Each question/answer would have to contain substantial specific information about events in the story, perhaps along with the page number in which the information is found. You can see how the process of formulating questions and answers *about the story* while scanning the list is making simultaneous use of instructional time: re-reading for a purpose, vocabulary review, and writing skills.

To assess receptive understanding, you could even include the targeted words within the questions that you ask students about the story, combining a reading content test with a vocabulary test. Tell the students that they can expect to find the words on their vocabulary list for *The Give*r embedded in the questions that will appear on the test, and that you won't be answering questions about word meanings during the test. You can structure those questions in such a way that you can tell by the answers whether the student understands the targeted words.

Involving Students in Assessment

Don't be afraid to have students participate in their own assessment. Have them select a certain number of words from a list, their readings, or their vocabulary journals and then actually make up their own tests, giving you the blank test the day before so that you can distribute it back to them on the day of the test. The method to this madness is that it is the process of making that test that allows for the processing necessary to learn the words. Students are likely to pick out the words that they think they already know, but they probably know these words only partially or only receptively. Taking "their own test with their own words" simply brings them closer to full productive knowledge.

Of course we don't suggest this for every assessment, but it is a good way to put students in control of their own vocabulary learning. And the experience of making up a test is valuable. By putting themselves in the shoes of test-makers, students develop insights about test formats that will give them an insider's familiarity. Familiarity with the test format relieves anxiety, which is one of several reasons why familiarity improves performance. In general, it's a good idea to have students try their hands at making up tests.

A student's skill at making up a test is another example of formative assessment: The student who composes a test that is unrealistically specific or overly general is showing you that she doesn't have a good idea about what test items look like. Therefore, how can she study? Students need to align their thinking with that of the test-maker, whether that be you, your department, or the makers of standardized tests like the SAT and ACT.

The instructional implication of this concept is that, since words are not known on an all-or-nothing basis, if we assess on an all-or-nothing basis (as with traditional assessments), then our assessment instruments are not sensitive enough to detect the extent to which students are learning about words.

Do Students Actually Retain and Use Their New Words?

Coming back to the four goals that we set forth at the beginning of this chapter—*expansion, retention, use, strategy*—we can see that the traditional vocabulary test addresses only the first one, expansion. But without retention and use, what good is expansion? If we want retention to go beyond the test, then we need to engage in continuous assessment. That is, to what extent do students indicate that they remember the words that they've learned? We'll assess their retention by monitoring their use of new words in various ways, over time.

The most practical, as well as the most student-centered, way to do this is to have the students note when they have used words that they have not used before in their writing. They can simply highlight such words. If you want a protocol that will build their awareness of vocabulary growth, you can have students note where their new words came from:

1. Was on our vocabulary list (highlight in yellow)
2. Was in my own word journal (highlight in green)

3.   Other: heard it in another class, heard it outside of school, read it on my own, don't know (highlight in pink)

This protocol is obviously not meant to be an exact science. Rather, it's meant to keep new words in play throughout the year and to make students more keenly aware of their word consciousness. You'll find that students do get excited, just as you do, when they use new words.

Assessment for Strategy

Part of our assessment should be focused on how well students know what to do when they meet an unfamiliar word. How skilled are they at using context clues? What about word components, especially Latin and Greek roots that allow us to make valuable connections to related words? Good vocabulary detectives use a variety of strategies to figure out unfamiliar words.

Good vocabulary detectives look around the word for context clues, and their search is not limited to the sentence in which the word appears: they use clues from all of the surrounding sentences. And good vocabulary detectives look inside the words for familiar components. But it is both of these strategies, working together, that begin to unlock meaning. Good vocabulary detectives are also patient, realizing that an unfamiliar word may take on clearer meaning as it is repeated in the text. Of course, good vocabulary detectives also know when it's time to look a word up in a dictionary or glossary *and* they know how to select among several definitions the one that suits the context.

Summative Assessments

Are you looking to measure vocabulary growth, vocabulary skills, or vocabulary knowledge? Measuring vocabulary knowledge is straightforward: How many words in a given domain does the student know? It's so easy to give a multiple choice test that gives information about vocabulary knowledge, so why would we bother to do anything else?

The reason why we would bother to assess vocabulary growth and vocabulary skills and not just vocabulary knowledge is that testing vocabulary knowledge alone doesn't tell us much about what the student has learned and can do as a result of our instruction. How do we know which of the words on the multiple choice test the student already knew before we came along? How do we know the extent to which the words have moved along the continuum from being completely unknown to being completely known? How do we know the extent to which the student's knowledge of the word goes beyond the knowledge required to get the test item correct? Because vocabulary knowledge is not an all-or-nothing thing, we can't rest assured that tests that measure vocabulary in an all-or-nothing way are all that informative.

We can only assess for vocabulary growth by knowing where the student began. That requires either a pretest/posttest protocol or some kind of self-assessment by the student.

We can assess for vocabulary skills by having students demonstrate the ability to analyze words through their recognizable components. The following fourteen words contain enough word components to produce 14,000 words in a collegiate dictionary, many thousands more in an unabridged dictionary. This list is commonly called "The 14 Words that Make All the Difference" (www.lexfiles.com).

precept	monograph	reproduction
detain	epilogue	indisposed
intermittent	aspect	oversufficient
offer	uncomplicated	mistranscribe
insist	nonextended	

A good assessment of a student's ability to use the strategy of word analysis is one that requires:

1. Naming the components of these words
2. Telling what the components mean
3. Generating a list of other words having these components

Conclusion

Assessment for vocabulary is not straightforward. It is certainly not a matter of giving a multiple choice or matching test for a word list. Shallow word knowledge, defined as the ability to pick out a definition that appears amid other definitions, is not the only indicator of a student's vocabulary development.

For vocabulary assessment to be authentic and informative, we need to make it ongoing, requiring the cumulative and sustained use of words that are new to the student's productive vocabulary. We need both formative and summative assessments for vocabulary that consider a student's vocabulary growth and the student's ability to use strategies to confront unfamiliar words.

Appendix A: Generic Academic Vocabulary

Set One: Words that indicate the requirements of a task
analyze (analyzing, analyzed, analysis, analytical, analytically)
annotate (annotation, annotated, annotating)
apply (application, applying, applier, applicable)
assert (assertion, asserting, asserted, assertive)
assess (assessing, assessed, assessment)
clarify (clarification, clarifying, clarified)
coherent (coherence, coherently)
comment (commentary, commenting, commented)
concise (conciseness)
convince (convincing, convinced)
critique (critic, critiquing, critiqued)
debate (debater, debating, debated, debatable)
describe (description, describing, described, descriptive, descriptively)
determine (determining, determined, determination)
discuss (discussion, discussing, discussed)
dissuade (dissuading, dissuaded)
employ (employment, employing, employed)
espouse (espousal, espousing, espoused)
estimate (estimation, estimating, estimated)
evaluate (evaluation, evaluator, evaluating, evaluated, evaluative)
explain (explanation, explaining, explained, explainable)
extrapolate (extrapolation, extrapolating, extrapolated)
identify (identification, identifying, identified, identifiable)
implement (implementation, implementing, implemented)
interpret (interpretation, interpreting, interpreted, interpretive)
overview
persuade (persuasion, persuading, persuaded, persuasive, persuasively)
precise (precision)
refute (refutation, refuting, refuted)
review (reviewer, reviewing, reviewed)
specify (specifics, specifying, specified, specifically)
stipulate (stipulation, stipulating, stipulated)
summary (summarize, summarizing, summarizing)
support (supporter, supporting, supported, supportive, supportively)
thorough (thoroughness)

well-developed
well-organized

Set Two: Words that establish relationships within units of information

according to
accordingly
aforementioned
afterwards
albeit
although
arguably
as follows
as such
because of
by means of
compared (to)
conclusive
coupled with
decidedly
despite
due to
even so
even though
except for

foregoing
furthermore
greater than
hence however
in accordance with
in conjunction with
in contrast (to)
in fact
in relation to; relative to
in spite of
in this regard
inasmuch as
less than
lest
likewise
moreover
nevertheless
notwithstanding
owing to
per se

regarding
regardless
respectively
save (to mean except)
set forth
similarly
such as
the following
therefore
thus
unless
whence
whereas
whereby
wherefore
wherein
with regard to
with the exception of

Set Three: Words about space and divisions of space

adjacent
area
arena
array
bilateral (bilaterally)
continuum
dimension
external (externally)
facet
internal (internally)
intersection (inter-
   sect, intersecting,
   intersected)

lateral (laterally)
linear
orientation (orient, ori-
   enting, oriented)
parameters
permeate (permeating,
   permeated)
pervasive (pervasively)
precinct
proximity (proximal)
realm
region (regional,
   regionally)

scope
section
sector
spatial (spatially)
spectrum
throughout
unilateral

Set Four: Words that are about how we think about a topic

acknowledge (acknowledgement, acknowledging, acknowledged)

assume (assumption, assuming, assumed)

deductive reasoning

essential (essentially)

fundamental (fundamentally)

given (noun)

imply (implication, implying, implied)

inductive reasoning

infer (inference, inferring, inferred)

intuition (intuitive, intuitively)

objective (objectivity, objectively)

overarching

perspective

premise

process of elimination

rudimentary (rudiment)

subjective (subjectivity, subjectively)

tentative (tentatively)

theme (thematic, thematically)

theory (theorize, theorizing, theorized, theoretical)

Set Five: Words about organization

breakdown

category (categorize, categorizing, categorized, categorical)

chapter

classification (classify, classifying, classified)

complement (complementary)

complex (complexity)

component

compound (compounding, compounded)

consist (consistency, consisting, consisted, consistent)

constitute (constitution, constituent, constituting, constituted)

contain (container, containing, contained)

dependent (dependant, depend, depending, depended)

design (designer, designee, designing, designed)

dissect (dissecting, dissected)

dominate (domination, dominating, dominated, dominant)

encompass (encompassing, encompassed)

exclude (exclusion, excluding, excluded, exclusionary, exclusive)

framework

hierarchy (hierarchical)

include (inclusion, including, included, inclusive)

independent (independence, independently)

layer

mainstream

matrix

mutual (mutually)

organize/reorganize (organization, organizing, organized, organic)

portion

proportion (proportional)

ratio

reciprocal (reciprocate, reciprocating, reciprocated)

section (sectional)

set

subordinate (subordinating, subordinated)

subset

supplement (supplemental)

taxonomy

unit

Set Six: Words about ideas

abstract (abstraction)

alternative (alternate, alternating, alternated)

comprehend (comprehension, comprehending, comprehended, comprehensive)

concept (conception, conceive, conceiving, conceived)

conjecture (conjecturing, conjectured)

generate (generation, generating, generated, generative)

hypothesis (hypothesize, hypothesizing, hypothesized)

hypothetical

issue (issuance, issuing, issued)

literal (literally)

metaphorical (metaphor)

paradox (paradoxical, paradoxically)

perceive (perception, perceiving, perceived, perceptive)

philosophy (philosophical)

relative (relatively)

research

resource (resourceful)

source

symbol (symbolic)

theme

thesis

Set Seven: Words about cause and effect

affect (affecting, affected)

consequence (consequential, consequentially)

contributing factor

effect (effective)

impact (impacting, impacted)

interact (interaction, interacting, interacted, interactive)

mitigating factor

respond (response, responding, responded)

result (resulting, resulted)

stimulate (stimulus, stimulating, stimulated)

Set Eight: Words about process

assemble (assembling, assembled)

covert (covertly)

emergent (emergency, emerging, emerged)

facilitate (facilitating, facilitated)

formative (formatively)

formula

formulate (formulating, formulated)

hamper (hampering, hampered)

hinder (hindering, hindered)

innovate (innovation, innovating, innovated)

latent (latently)

manipulate (manipulation, manipulating, manipulated)

method (methodical, methodically)

overt (overtly)
process (procedure, processing, processed, procedural)
protocol
strategy (strategic, strategically)
technique

Set Nine: Words about amounts and degrees
crucial
deficient (deficiency)
maximum (maximize, maximizing, maximized)
minimum (minimize, minimizing, minimal)
negligible
proportion (proportionate)
range (ranging, ranged)
significance (significant, significantly; insignificant, insignificantly)
substantial (substantially)
substantive (substantively)
sufficient (sufficiently)
unsubstantial (unsubstantially)
volume

Set Ten: Words about time and order
chronological (chronology, chronologically)
concurrent (concurrently)
contemporary
current (currently)
index
initial (initiate, initiating, initiated)
intermittent (intermittently)
interval
overlapping (overlap, overlapped)
previous (previously)
prior
sequence (sequential)
simultaneous (simultaneously)
subsequent (subsequently)
transient (transience)

Set Eleven: Words about systems
aspect
attribute (attributing, attributed, attributable)
core

cycle (cyclical)
device
establishment (establish, establishing, establish)
feature (featuring, featured)
function (functional)
hierarchy (hierarchical)
infrastructure
institution (institute, instituting, instituted)
integral (integrity, integrate, integrating, integrated)
mechanism
orchestrate (orchestrating, orchestrated)
paradigm
regulate (regulation, regulated, regulatory)
trigger (triggering, triggered)

Set Twelve: Words about change and stability

accelerate (acceleration, accelerating, accelerated)
cease (cessation, ceasing, unceasing, ceased)
collapse (collapsing, collapsed)
convert (conversion, converting, converted)
decrease (decreasing, decreased)
deteriorate (deterioration, deteriorating, deteriorated)
diminish (diminishing, diminished)
distort (distorting, distorted)
dynamic (dynamics, dynamism)
evolve (evolution, evolving, evolved)
expand (expansion, expanding, expanded, expansive)
flexible
fluctuate (fluctuating, fluctuated)
increase (increasing, increased)
maintain (maintenance, maintaining, maintained)
modify (modification, modifier, modifying, modified)
pivot (pivoting, pivoted, pivotal)
plateau
radical
regenerate (regenerating, regenerated, regenerative)
restructure (restructuring, restructured)
reverse (reversal, reversing, reversed)
revert (reversion, reverting, reverted)
revive (revival, reviving, revived)
revolve (revolution, revolving, revolved, revolutionary)
rotate (rotator, rotation, rotating, rotated)

stable (stabilizer, destabilizer, stability, instability, stabilize, stabilizing, stabi-
   lized, unstable)
sustain (sustenance, sustaining, sustained, sustainable)
transform (transformer, transformation, transforming, transformed,
   transformative)
uniform (uniformity)

Appendix B: Latin and Greek Word Components

The English language has hundreds of Latin word stems from which we derive thousands of words. Here is a partial list of some of the most accessible and useful ones for students:

cede, ceed, cess: to go, to yield	accede, access, concede, concession exceed, excessive necessary, necessitate process, procession recede, recession secession, succession
clud, clus, clos: to close	clause cloister closet conclude, conclusion enclose exclude, exclusion include, inclusion occlude, occlusion preclude, preclusion recluse, reclusive seclude, seclusion
cur, curs: to run	current, currency cursive, cursor cursory discursive incur, incursion occur, occurrence recur, recursive, recurrent
duct, duce: to lead, to pull	abduct, abductor, abduction aqueduct conduct duct, ductile deduce, deduct, deduction induce, induct, inducement, induction produce, product, producer, productive reduce, reductive seduce, seduction, seductive, transducer

fac, fic: to do, to make	de facto
	faction
	fact, factor, factory
	fiction, fictitious, manufacture
fer, phor: to carry	confer, conference
	conifer
	defer, deference, deferential
	differ, difference, different, differential, differentiate
	infer, inference, inferential
	metaphor, metaphorical
	offer
	phosphorescence
	refer, reference, referent
	suffer, sufferance, insufferable
	transfer, transference
flec, flex: to bend	deflect, deflection
	flexible, flexibility
	genuflect, genuflection
	inflect, inflection
	reflect, reflection
flu, flux: flow	affluence, affluent
	confluence
	effluent
	flue, fluent, fluency
	influence, influx
	reflux, suffuse, superfluous
gress, grad: to step	aggression, aggressive, congress, congressional, degrade
	egress
	grade, gradient, graduate
	ingress
	progress, progressive, progression, regress, regressive, regression
	retrograde
ject: to throw	adjective, abject
	deject, dejection, inject, injection
	object, objective, objectify
	subject, subjective
	trajectory
lat: side	lateral, bilateral, unilateral
	latitude
	relate, relative, relationship

mit, miss: to send	admit
	permit
	remit, emit, omit, transmit, admission, permission, remission, emission, omission, transmission, mission, missionary, submit, submissive, submission
morph: shape	morpheme, morphology, amorphous, polymorphous, ectomorph, mesomorph, endomorph, metamorphosis
mot: to move	motility, motivate, motive, remote, demote, promote
nom, nym: to name	nominate, denominator, nominal, ignominy, nomenclature, synonym, acronym, homonym
pel, pul: to drive	impel, propel, repel, dispel, expel, compel, impulse, propeller, propulsion, repulsive, expulsion, compulsion
plic, plex: to fold	complicate, complicit, implicate, explicate, explicit, implicit
	accomplice, supplicate, duplicate, replicate
	complex
port: to carry	transport, import, export, portable, deport, report, support, port, opportunity
pos, pon: to put or place	position, depose, deposition, disposition, repose, suppose, expose, exposure, exposition, expository, impose, imposition
reg, rect: straight	rectangle, regular, rectify, erect, rectitude, correct, direct
script, scribe: write	transcript, scripture, conscription, prescription, subscription, prescribe, transcribe, subscribe, proscribe, inscribe, inscription, describe, description, manuscript
sect, sec: to cut	section, secular, bisect, dissect, intersect, transect, sector, secant
ten, tin, tain, tang, tex, tec, tac, teg: to touch, to hold	ascertain
	attack
	attain
	attend, attention
	contain, containment
	contend, contention
	contingent, contingency
	detain, detention, detainee
	extend, extensive, extension
	integer, integral, integrity, intact
	intend, intensive, intention

ten, tin, tain, tang,	maintain, maintenance
tex, tec, tac, teg:	pretend, pretense, pretension
to touch, to hold	pretext
(cont'd)	retain, retention
	sustain, sustenance
	tactile, tacky, tact, texture
	tenure, tenant, tenet,
	texture, text, tangential
tract: to drag,	attract, attractive, attraction, contract, contraction
to draw	detract
	distract, distraction, extract, extraction, intractable
	protract, protractor, protracted
	retract, retraction
	subtract, subtraction
	traction, tractor, tractable
veh, vect: to carry	convection
	vector
	vehicle
vert, vers: to turn	averse, aversion, avert
	adversity
	converse, controversy, convert, conversion
	diverse, diversion, divert
	inverse, inversion
	obverse
	reverse, reversion, revert
	subvert, subversive, subversion
	versatile, verse

The stems above usually appear in the middle of the word. Here are a few more that usually appear at the beginning of words. Yet, they can't be considered prefixes because they are an integral part of the word. (A prefix would have to be removable from the word, leaving the word intact, such as *reread, preview.*)

ambi, amphi: both	ambivalent, ambidextrous, amphibian, amphibious
dyna: power	dynamic, dynamo, dynasty
per: through	permeate, permeable, perspire, perforate, persuade
bene: good	benefit, *note bene*, benefactor, benevolent, beneficiary, benign
mal: bad	malnutrition, malcontentment, malefactor, malice, malicious, malignant
meta: beyond, change	metamorphosis, metacognition, metaphysical, metaphor, metabolism

mut: change	mutable, mutation, immutable, mutiny
syn: together	synthesis, synchronize, syntax, synergy
con, com: together	convene, compress, contemporary, converge, compact, conduct, confluence, committee, communal, constituent, component
trans: across	transcontinental, transient, transdermal, transitory, transition, transit, transport, transfer
equi: balance	equal, equilateral, equidistant, equilibrium

The prefixes below indicate spatial relationships and are frequently found in academic language.

ecto, exo: outside	exoskeleton
extra: in addition	extrapolate, extraterrestrial
inter: between	interaction, interactive
	intercoastal
	interpersonal
peri: around	perimeter
	periscope
	perinatal
super, supra: beyond	supernova
	superfluous

When you present the roots, always be sure to have at least one familiar word in the list of derivatives, so that the student can connect new information to known information. If all of the derivatives are new words, the student will just think: "Here are a bunch of words that I don't know."

And note that teaching word components has the added benefit of teaching spelling clusters. Students become better spellers when they see clusters, rather than thinking that English words are spelled at random.

In addition, we have many words that populate academic text whose Latin or Greek origin is expressed at the ends of words (but not as suffixes). These words are particularly common in mathematics and science, and they are also common in social studies.

-us	apparatus, bacillus/bacilli, locus/loci, focus/foci, fungus/fungi, radius/radii, sinus, stimulus/stimuli, syllabus/syllabi, terminus, virus
-um, as the singular	bacterium/bacteria, datum/data, medium/media,
-a, as the plural	referendum/referenda
-ex, -ix	apex, appendix/appendices, index/indices, matrix/matrices, vortex/vortices

| -is | analysis, epiglottis, glottis, metropolis, synopsis |
| -on | criterion/criteria, electron, horizon, neutron, phenomenon, polyhedron, tetrahedron |

Common Phonemic Blends in Greek-Based Words

The Greek-based words are extremely important in academic understandings, and the way that they are spelled can be off-putting to inexperienced readers. Certain letter clusters typify Greek-based words and special attention should be paid to them because of their usefulness and possible unfamiliarity to deficient readers:

ph: Words that have the *ph* combination having the sound of *f* are always Greek-based and deserving of special attention. Examples: *phonics, phonetic, alphabet, physical, physics, graphic, photosynthesis, geography*

-y: When a word has a *y* as its second letter, that word is Greek-based and deserves special attention. Examples: *mystery, dynamics, cycle, gyrate, hypothesis, lyrics, symmetry, tyrant*

ch: *psychology, chaos, chemical, chroma, chromosome*

sci: *science, conscience, conscientious*

Other words of Greek origin that deserve special attention are words that end in *-ology*, words with the unvoiced *th* sound (*theme, thesis*), words ending in *-sis* (*crisis, thesis, synthesis*), those having the *kn* or *gn* that have to do with knowledge (*knowledge, acknowledge, agnostic*).

Appendix C: Shallow vs. Deep Processing

Shallow Processing

We want you to experience what it is like to try to learn new words in the traditional manner, requiring a shallow level of processing, contrasted to the type of exposure we advocate in this book. To that end, we have chosen ten uncommon words, most of which you probably do not know, and given you their definitions. Study the following list to memorize its contents. If you wish, read the list several times, concentrating only on the words and their meanings. As English teachers, you may very well have more sophisticated tools and techniques that you would normally use; however, your students probably don't. So do your best to be like them in order to replicate their experience with traditional vocabulary instruction:

1. *pogonip:* a dense winter fog containing frozen particles that is formed in deep mountain valleys of the western United States
2. *oscitant:* yawning (from drowsiness); inattentive; negligent
3. *soporose:* sleepy; in an unusually deep sleep
4. *lychnobite:* one who works at night and sleeps during the day
5. *sternutation:* the act of sneezing or a sneeze
6. *debouch:* to emerge or issue from a narrow area into the open
7. *clinquant:* glittering, especially with gold or tinsel
8. *exiguous:* extremely scanty; meager
9. *aposematic (ap-uh-suh-MAT-ik):* serving as a warning or alarm, used in zoology
10. *acescent:* turning sour; slightly sour

Once you have finished studying the words, turn to Appendix D for the first round of testing. We ask that you take the tests now and, if possible, wait two to three days, without reviewing the words, and take the same tests again. Do not continue to the next section until you have taken both sets of tests.

Deeper Processing

Now we want you to experience the difference between shallow tasks, such as memorizing definitions, and tasks that require deeper processing. Read through the following material carefully, answering the questions and filling in the blanks as required. You have to imagine that you are in a classroom and that some of the items provoke discussion:

- **pogonip:** a dense winter fog containing frozen particles that is formed in deep mountain valleys of the western United States
  - This word comes from a Shoshone Indian word for white death.
  - For a **pogonip** to form, conditions must be just right: the humidity has to be near 100% and the temperature needs to be below freezing.
  - The fog is very dangerous for two reasons:
    - It is very easy to become lost in it—it is so thick that you can barely see your hand in front of your face.
    - Breathing it can damage your lungs.
  - The ending of the word sounds as if it came from *nippy*. It might help you to remember it by remembering that, if there is a pogonip, you shouldn't go outside: No go—nip(py).
  - I would ask you to draw a picture of it, but a blank white sheet of paper is probably the best representation possible. Just hold a piece of paper in front of your face, and you'll know what a pogonip looks like.
- **oscitant:** yawning (from drowsiness); inattentive; negligent
  - Comes from Latin
    - *os* meaning *mouth*
    - *citare* meaning *to move*
  - Have you ever seen students whom you could describe as oscitant?
  - Where were you the last time you were oscitant?
  - Dr. Bill Long noted the following: "This word would eventually be picked up by Protestant divines in the 17th century and used figuratively to describe congregants who had lost their zeal for Christian faith."[3]
  - Imagine yourself yawning. How can you "fit" this word into the act of yawning?
  - Analogy: **oscitant** is to **mouth** as **expressive** is to _____ .
- **soporose:** sleepy; in an unusually deep sleep
  - Comes from Latin *sopor* meaning *a deep sleep*.
  - If one is **soporose**, then one could be said to be in a **stupor**.
  - What characters in literature were **soporose** at some point?
  - What sound would you associate with **soporose**? (Snoring: z-z-z-z)
  - Similar words?

[3]Source: http://www.drbilllong.com/2006Words/Motins.html

- Dissimilar words?
- Analogy: **soporose** is to **alcohol** as **agitated** is to _____ .
- Create a graphic image that represents the meaning of **soporose**.

♦ **lychnobite:** one who works at night and sleeps during the day
  - Comes from Greek
    - *lychnos* meaning *lamp*
    - *bios* meaning *life*
  - Sounds almost like a conversational exchange:
    - person A: "Lick?"
    - person B: "No, bite!"
  - Analogy: A **lychnobite** is to **people** as an **owl** is to _____ .
  - Would you consider yourself to be a **lychnobite**? What about most of your friends?
  - During the day, most people are awake. What word (from previously studied words) might describe a **lychnobite** at noontime?
  - What other people might be described as **lychnobites**? (Anyone who works the graveyard shift in a factory, hospital, etc.)

♦ **sternutation:** the act of sneezing or a sneeze
  - From the Latin word for *sneeze* (*sternutatio*)
  - What would you think a *sternutator* might be? I'll show you the answer in the final bullet.
  - The *sternum* is your breastbone. Is it involved at all in **sternutation**?
  - If you do not cover your mouth and nose during **sternutation**, you may receive a *stern* rebuke from people around you.
  - What should you say after someone else's **sternutation**—and why?
  - Analogy: **sternutation** is to **nose** as **digestion** is to _____ .
  - How do English speakers spell the sound that one makes during **sternutation**? Do all languages represent sneezing with a similar sound?
  - A *sternutator* is anything that makes you sneeze.

♦ **debouch:** to emerge or issue from a narrow area into the open
  - Comes from French
    - *de* meaning *out of*
    - *bouche* meaning *mouth*
  - Examples of usage:
    - The Mississippi **debouches** into the Gulf.
    - The army **debouched** into the valley.
  - What other examples can you come up with?
  - Have you ever been a part of a group that **debouched**?
  - Analogy: **debouch** is to **fire hose** as **sternutation** is to _____ .

♦ **clinquant:** glittering, especially with gold or tinsel
  - Comes from French *clinquer* meaning *to clink*

- Why is **clinquant** onomatopoetic?
- Examples of usage:
  - A **clinquant** Christmas tree.
  - A **clinquant** evening gown.
- What other examples can you come up with?
- Synonym(s)?
- Antonym(s)?
- Shakespeare used it in *Henry VIII*: "Today the French,/All clinquant, all in gold, like heathen gods,/Shone down the English"
- What is the relationship between **clinquant** and **bling**?
- Have you ever worn anything that could be called **clinquant**?

♦ **exiguous:** extremely scanty; meager
  - Comes from Latin *exiguus* meaning *strict, exact*
  - Synonym(s)?
  - Antonym(s)?
  - Would you consider your own personal budget to be **exiguous**?
  - Where might one expect to eat **exiguous** meals?
  - Draw a graphic image that represents **exiguous**.
  - Would **exiguous** be a good word to describe a teacher's salary?

♦ **aposematic**: serving as a warning or alarm, used in zoology
  - Comes from Greek
    - *apo* meaning *away from*
    - *sema* meaning *sign*
  - The word apogee means the farthest or highest point, the culmination.
  - How does apo- fit in this meaning?
  - What other words can you think of that begin with *sema*?
  - What creatures have coloration that is **aposematic**?
  - Do you think that sounds in nature could be aposematic?
  - Analogy: **aposematic** is to **skunk** as **camouflage** is to _____ .
  - Although **aposematic** isn't commonly used outside of the animal and plant kingdoms, how could the color red be considered **aposematic** in our society?

♦ **acescent:** turning sour; slightly sour
  - Comes from Latin *acescens* meaning *to turn sour*
  - What is the main clue you use to decide whether or not milk is **acescent**?
  - Would it be fair to say that the **ace** (main) clue that you use to remember this word is **scent**?
  - What else could be characterized as **acescent**?
  - **Acescent** is not normally used to describe a person. If it were, however, what could cause someone to become **acescent**?

- Related words: acrid, vinegar, acid, acute
- Analogy: **acescent** is to **vinegar** as _____ is to **vanilla**.

Now turn to Appendix D and take the two tests again. Then wait two or more days—without looking at the material—and take the tests one more time. Contrast the experience and the results from your initial exposure and testing.

Appendix D: Vocabulary Quizzes

Part I: Matching
Write the letter of the word on the left next to its definition on the right:

A. debouch	1. _____	very soundly asleep
B. soporose	2. _____	sparkling
C. exiguous	3. _____	well short of enough
D. acescent	4. _____	a type of fog
E. sternutation	5. _____	becoming sour
F. oscitant	6. _____	yawning
G. clinquant	7. _____	a night owl
H. pogonip	8. _____	acting as a forewarning
I. lychnobite	9. _____	a sneeze
J. aposematic	10. _____	to spread out from an opening

The answer key follows the next test, but please do not check your answers until you complete the fill-in-the-blank quiz on the next page.

Part II: Fill in the Blanks
Write the letter of the word that best fills in each blank:

A. debouch   *B. soporose*   *C. exiguous*   *D. acescent*   *E. sternutation*
F. oscitant   *G. clinquant*   *H. pogonip*   *I. lychnobite*   *J. aposematic*

1. We poured the _____ milk down the drain.
2. After an hour, many people in the audience were _____ .
3. While driving through California, we encountered a _____ and had to pull over until it dissipated.
4. After retiring, many people find that their budgets are so _____ that they cannot live comfortably.
5. Rip Van Winkle was in a _____ state for twenty years.
6. The _____ Christmas tree was the center of attention as soon as you entered the room.
7. I was asleep by 10:00 pm; my wife, however, was a _____ .
8. Ragweed and pollen causes frequent _____ in many allergy sufferers.
9. Many rivers _____ into the Gulf of Mexico.
10. The gathering clouds were _____ of rough weather ahead.

If you have not gone through the deeper levels of processing, you are finished—check your answers. The answer key for both quizzes follows Part III's exercise.

Part III

Use each of these words in a meaningful sentence, following the guidelines in Chapter 3:

A. debouch   B. soporose   C. exiguous   D. acescent   E. sternutation
F. suppurate   G. clinquant   H. pogonip   I. lychnobite   J. aposematic

Answer Keys

#	Part I: Matching	Part II: Blanks
1.	B	D
2.	G	F
3.	C	H
4.	H	C
5.	D	B
6.	F	G
7.	I	I
8.	J	E
9.	E	A
10.	A	J

Appendix E: Phrasal Verbs and Their Latinate Counterparts

Phrasal verbs, two-part verbs that are common in English conversation, generally correspond to Latinate verbs. In academic discourse, we find the Latinate versions of the phrasal verbs. Because the Latinate verbs occur less frequently than the phrasal verbs in ordinary conversation, students are often unfamiliar with them. However, the fact that the students are probably familiar with the concepts expressed in the phrasal verbs facilitates the transition from the known to the new.

To accelerate the process of expanding students' vocabulary, develop a habit of scaffolding in your speech: Use *both* the phrasal verb *and* its Latinate counterpart as you speak to students.

Another important thing about phrasal verbs is that they represent particular difficulties for students whose native language is not English. This difficulty arises from the fact that the phrasal verb means something other than the meaning of the two separate words that comprise it. And phrasal verbs are extremely common in casual conversation, so they are important to know, but the student whose knowledge of English is unsteady might not know them yet, and cannot look them up word by word. To make matters worse, native speakers take phrasal verbs for granted because they are so common. So, if we are native speakers ourselves, we might glide right over the phrasal verbs that pepper our speech, not even realizing that the English language learner is baffled by them.

Finally, phrasal verbs represent an additional challenge when it comes to the students' vocabulary in writing: Phrasal verbs are, by their nature, informal. Academic writing is, by its nature, formal, calling for the Latinate "translation" rather than the phrasal verbs, which are, as we say, in a "lower register." This last point affects native speakers of English whose written vocabulary remains in that lower register.

For all of these reasons, we offer this partial list of phrasal verbs and their Latinate counterparts. We've selected the most common verbs that are used to create phrasal verbs.

Base Verb	*Phrasal Verb*	*Latinate Counterpart*
break	break down break up break out break through	collapse; analyze discontinue erupt transcend

Base Verb	Phrasal Verb	Latinate Counterpart
bring	bring out bring in bring together	evoke include synthesize
call	call off call back call in call on	cancel recall request; summon visit; select
catch	catch up with catch on	apprehend; equalize comprehend
come	come over come up come down come back come up with come across come off as	visit ascend descend return; revisit devise, invent; develop encounter appear
count	count on count up	rely calculate
cut	cut out cut back on; cut down	eliminate; excise minimize; reduce; decrease; restrict; diminish
fill	fill in; fill out fill in for	complete substitute
get	get along; get by get through get in get out	survive; exist; sustain complete admit exit; extricate
go	go through go back go on go away	experience regress; review continue disappear; recede

Base Verb	Phrasal Verb	Latinate Counterpart
hold	hold off hold on hold out hold in	postpone defer offer; proffer retain
leave	leave out leave in leave off	omit retain; maintain discontinue; omit
let	let down let in	disappoint admit; accept
look	look forward to look up to	anticipate respect; admire
make	make up make fun of make out	reconcile; compensate; devise; prevaricate; fabri- cate; manufacture deride discern; interpret
put	put away put down put out	deposit disparage; settle expose; release
run	run into run down run up run out on	encounter exhaust accumulate desert
set	set up set back	establish delay
take	take up take in take out	commence absorb extract
throw	throw up throw out throw in	regurgitate discard; eject contribute; surrender

Base Verb	Phrasal Verb	Latinate Counterpart
turn	turn in turn out turn down turn up	submit eventuate; result reject appear
wear	wear out	exhaust
work	work out	exercise; resolve
hold	work up work through	calculate resolve
wrap	wrap up wrap in	complete enclose

Appendix F: Model Activity for Vocabulary Expansion: Let's Get Kids Talking About Words

Because language is a social activity, it's very important to create a sociable environment for the processing of vocabulary. When students are strengthening their vocabulary skills, bringing their understandings of partially known words to the next level, they shouldn't be working alone, quietly. They should be in a cooperative learning situation where they can engage the words through multiple learning modalities: visual, kinesthetic, auditory, and tactile.

What follows is a cooperative learning activity that engages students in the kind of word-learning that reinforces what they already know while leveraging known words by connecting them to related words.

Activity: Apple Trees
Purpose
The purpose of this activity is to have students work together to create classroom visuals that illustrate relationships among words having the same root. This activity also reinforces spelling by setting up associations among words having a common root. By displaying the words, you are providing important visual reinforcement.

Suggested Procedure
We're using the metaphor of an apple tree to show how words are related. We already use the language of botany (roots, stems, branching) to talk about etymology. Have students work together to draw the apple trees. The words go inside the apples; the letters that the words have in common go on the bottom of the tree, as its root. (Note that in some groupings, as in the first one, the common root would be *grav* even though the word *grief* does not have all four letters. You may have to explain how the letters *f* and *v* are often found in related words because one is simply the unvoiced version of the other.) Have students first make an educated guess as to the meaning of the root by trying to figure out what all of the words have in common. At first, they may be mystified, but the more talking they do about the words, the more the etymological foundation will reveal itself. Have them confirm their educated guess by looking up any one of the words in a collegial dictionary.

There are sixty-three word sets, so the apple tree diagrams should be small enough for all of them to be displayed, yet large enough to be read from all seats in the room. Divide the words among the groups rather than trying to have all of the students work through the entire list.

Encourage students to find cognates in other Romance languages and to include them on the apple tree.

Scaffolding

If students are having difficulty, you might want to provide clues about the roots, such as an index of the roots, along with their definitions, that the students have to match to the word groups for which they are responsible. But don't have them go straight to the dictionary to locate the root before attempting to make an educated guess. Doing so would result in an exercise in copying rather than in thinking cooperatively and communicating.

Advancement

The Dictionary of Latin and Greek Origins: A Comprehensive Guide to the Classical Origins of English Words lists many other low-frequency words for these roots. It also gives you words that look similar, but do not, in fact, emanate from the given root. Ask students to include a nonrelated word on their drawings, but be sure that the nonrelated word is not on the apple tree. For example, the word *prepare* is not related to the words having the root *par* meaning equal, such as *disparage, compare, parity, disparity.*

1. gravity, grief, engrave, gravel
2. specific, spectator, special, inspector
3. elevator, alleviate, levee, relieve
4. associate, social, society, antisocial
5. congregation, egregious, segregate, gregarious
6. consecutive, segue, sequence, consequence
7. auditorium, auditory, audio, audition
8. primate, primitive, primary, prime number
9. attract, retracted, tractor, subtraction
10. radio, radius, radial, radiate
11. application, duplicate, multiply, complex
12. experiment, permeate, permeable, permanent
13. science, conscience, conscious, omniscient
14. amphibian, ambidextrous, ambivalent, ambiguous
15. magnet, magnify, magnificent, magnitude
16. thermometer, thermonuclear, thermos, isotherm
17. habitat, inhabit, habitation, habit
18. reflect, inflection, deflected, genuflect
19. inspire, perspiration, respiration, spirit
20. conversion, versatile, invert, reversal
21. obtuse, obstruct, occlude, obstinate
22. strict, restriction, district, stringent

23. tension, intense, tangent, intangible
24. median, medial, medium, immediate
25. denominator, nominate, denomination, polynomial
26. intersect, bisect, section, dissect
27. mutation, commutative, commute, immutable
28. decide, precise, incision, excise
29. president, resident, reside, residual
30. organize, organism, organic, organ
31. positive, position, impose, pose
32. bilateral, quadrilateral, unilateral, latitude
33. negative, negate, negligible, negligent
34. symmetry, sympathy, symphony, synergy
35. sympathy, empathy, pathology, pathetic
36. distributive, attribute, contribution, tribute
37. inscription, manuscript, scripture, ascribe
38. response, correspond, sponsor, responsibility
39. anticipate, precipitation, incipient, recipient
40. context, texture, text, intact
41. affect, effect, infection, affectionate
42. evaluate, value, valid, value
43. essence, essential, necessary, process
44. illustrate, lucid, elucidate, luster
45. collect, recollect, lecture, elect
46. project, rejection, trajectory, conjecture
47. refer, transference, inference, conference
48. satisfy, saturated, sated, insatiable
49. opportunity, optician, opera, obvious
50. genesis, generation, degenerate, regenerate
51. contain, retain, maintenance, remainder
52. appropriate, proper, property, proprietary
53. inform, format, formal, formulate
54. definition, refine, infinity, finite
55. temporary, contemporary, temporal, temperature
56. depend, suspended, pendulum, independent
57. revoke, vocabulary, provocative, invocation
58. proficient, efficient, sufficient, fiction
59. labor, elaborate, laboratory, belabor
60. corporate, incorporate, corpus, corpuscle
61. sign, signify, significant, insignia
62. duct, introduce, deduction, inductive
63. polite, political, metropolitan, police

Appendix G: Anchor Activities for Vocabulary Development

The term *anchor activity* refers to meaningful engagements that students can do on their own or with each other, in or out of class. With differentiated instruction, students work at different rates, resulting in the need for anchor activities. Think of the following five criteria when you choose anchor activities for vocabulary development:

1. *Meaningful engagement:* Does the activity allow the student to produce or respond to the target words in as they are used in authentic communication? An example of an activity which, by itself, would not be considered meaningful engagement would be calling out "answers" to flash cards, whether the "answers" are definitions of a flashed word, or the target word being spoken in response to the flash of a definition or synonym.

   An example of a meaningful engagement would be for students to create a blog about a topic of interest and carry on an online conversation that is laced with target words. Even if the target words do sound forced, at least the student is combing through the new vocabulary in search of words that actually communicate their ideas.

2. *Recursivity:* Does the activity provide opportunity for revisiting words learned earlier? Remember that the goal is to grow productive vocabulary, not to learn a word only to have it fade in the mind because of disuse. A new word is like a weak muscle, and it must be exercised if it is expected to "be there" when needed to do a job. The two examples above (the flashcards and the blog) apply here as well.

3. *Imagination:* It's always a good day in class when students stretch their creative muscles. When students reach out to make new combinations, draw unexpected connections, find humor, and integrate the arts, durable learning is likely to result.

4. *Simplicity of administration:* Don't bite off more than you can chew in terms of manageability. Don't defeat yourself with excessive paperwork, complex assessment demands, or details that you just can't keep track of. Go slowly and keep it simple.

5. *Reinforcement of patterns:* Good language arts activities enlighten students about patterns of meaning, structure, and spelling. So it's a good idea to set up charts and tables for all students to see patterns clearly and to create them.

Don't worry if your anchor activity does not meet all of the criteria. Use them as guidelines, as any one of the criteria would indicate a worthwhile experience. Remember that what we're trying to move away from is rote memorization of a list of unrelated words.

Here's a short list of classroom applications that you can use as a starter kit for your anchor activities:

1. *Morphology charts:* Have lots of these available. Students can, at any point, plot words on the morphology charts. Morphology charts show patterns and the flexibility of a single word.
2. *Blogs:* Include a blogging feature on your classroom website (www .blogspot.com is a very user-friendly one. You'll need to feed it the e-mail addresses of your students who wish to participate. This creates an online space that is inaccessible to outsiders.) Post evocative questions that invite students to share their ideas while taking their new vocabulary out for a stroll in cyber-space.
3. *Word games and puzzles:* Crossword puzzles are an excellent way to develop the habit of thinking about the flexible meaning of words. They also reinforce spelling patterns. Students can create and find puzzles of varying degrees of difficulty, the most venerated being, of course, the *New York Times* (Will Shortz, editor). Despite the formidable reputation of the *New York Times'* puzzles, high school word lovers, working together, can certainly make a dent in it, especially on Mondays and Tuesdays, when Mr. Shortz is most merciful. For more accessible puzzles, explore www.puzzlemaker.com.
4. *Skits:* Students can put their vocabulary into service by writing and performing all kinds of skits, from lampoons to simulated interviews, newscasts, public service announcements, etc.
5. *Posters:* Give students the option to create clear and attractive posters that display the full array of a word's meaning. They might include related words, synonyms, antonyms, sentences, and pictures. Use these as classroom visuals to reinforce learning for the whole class and to advertise your commitment to interesting, useful words.
6. *Care and feeding of the personal word journal:* A personal word journal should be just as much a part of your class as the student's writing journal or reader response journal. It can be a dedicated segment of the larger English language arts journal and should reflect the student's own interests and needs regarding new words.

Worksheets, Graphic Organizers, Processing Guides: What's the Difference?

Throughout this book, we've been steering you away from such structures as worksheets, flashcards, matching columns, and drills. But we've been advocating things like graphic organizers, processing guides, and puzzles. What's the difference?

The important difference between what we're calling a worksheet and what we regard as a structure for durable learning is that the former tends to open the door very narrowly, inviting in one correct answer at a time, allowing for very little flexibility. The latter—whether it be called a graphic organizer or a processing chart—serves as a means through which students can express and expand what they know. Graphic organizers are powerful tools for learning, because they do something that fill-in-the-blank worksheets never do: allow for open thinking and the discovery of patterns. In a graphic organizer (such as a morphology chart), what's emphasized is the process; in a worksheet, what's emphasized is the single right answer. Additionally, graphic organizers can be used repeatedly, applied to different content because they are, in themselves, a pattern. They provide a closet for our ideas, a place where details fit with main ideas. Graphic organizers can be added to as students learn more; worksheets, when completed, invite no further elaboration or revisiting. Finally, all worksheets, when completed, will (ideally) look the same. Graphic organizers, when completed, will reflect the schema of individual learners.

Appendix H: Frequency of Occurrence

Frequency-of-occurrence lists have been around for decades, generated primarily by feeding millions of words of text taken from a wide variety of print sources (magazines, newspapers, novels, etc.) into computers so that they could sort and count the words. Averil Coxhead (2000) took it one important step further. She analyzed only academic texts and discovered that, after moving past the 2,000 most frequently occurring words, the next 570 words, the so-called Academic Word List (AWL), were *twice as likely* to show up as words in the next *1,000* frequently occurring words from a more broadly based sample. Her analysis, published in *TESOL Quarterly*, was aimed at helping non-native speakers (or their teachers) know what words to cover. However, the list is also very helpful for teachers of native English speakers. (The complete list can be found at http://language.massey.ac.nz/staff/awl/awlinfo.shtml.)

Frequency of occurrence lists divide words into **headwords** and **families**. A **headword** is the base form of the word—with no prefixes or suffixes. A **word family** is the headword and all of its derivatives. So, for example, *legal* would be a **headword**; forms such as *illegal, legally,* and *illegally* would be part of its **family**.

The Generic Academic Vocabulary (GAV) list in Appendix A shows headwords followed by derivations in parentheses. As we stated earlier, this list was not generated based on any scientific or statistical analysis; instead, it was created based on many years of classroom experience and exposure. However, the breakdown according to frequency of occurrence shows that it conforms very nicely to frequency of occurrence expectations:

Frequency of Occurrence	GAV	Cumulative
1–1,000	20%	20%
1,001-2000	3%	23%
AWL	51%	74%
Above AWL	26%	100%

The only surprise is that so many of the words on the GAV are hits in the first 1,000 words. The explanation leads us to an important aspect of vocabulary: word families can contain words that have different meanings from their headwords. Students might know *substance* (a word that appears in the first 1,000 most commonly occurring words), for example, but not be familiar with *substantive*, which is on the GAV.

Determining Frequency

So how did we determine where the words on the GAV fell within frequency of occurrence charts? The surprisingly simple process (thanks to Tom Cobb, the University of Montreal, and the Internet) is one that is useful any time you are deciding which words to target for explicit instruction or any time you want to know the complexity of the vocabulary of a reading passage. The following website does the magic: http://www.lextutor.ca/vp/eng

You can copy and paste any text into the existing window and click on the Submit button. The computer does the rest, giving you percentage breakdowns for frequency of occurrence, a color-coded version of your passage, and various lists. You could, for example, paste some text into the window and get a list of all of the words in that text that are on the AWL.

In our case, we stripped the list down to headwords only, deleted the prepositions and articles (a/an/the) that appeared in phrases such as *in spite of*, and pasted the remaining words into the window.

The site contains a number of interesting features that you might want to explore. Click on the Home link in the upper left-hand corner for a complete menu of options.

Appendix I: Correlation to the Common Core

Correlation of *Vocabulary at the Core's* Classroom Applications to the Common Core State Standards for English Language Arts, Grades K–12

The following table shows you how the Classroom Applications throughout this book meet the Common Core State Standards. Skill areas are abbreviated as follows: Language (L), Reading (R), Writing (W), and Speaking and Listening (SL).

Classroom Application	Anchor Standards for English Language Arts, Grades K–12	
Chapter 2		
Activity 1: Group Fill-In, p. 11	SL.1	Prepare for and participate effectively in a range of conversations and collaborations with diverse partners, building on other's ideas and expressing their own clearly and persuasively.
	L.4	Determine or clarify the meaning of unknown and multiple-meaning words and phrases by using context clues, analyzing meaningful word parts, and consulting general and specialized reference materials, as appropriate.
	L.5	Demonstrate understanding of figurative language, word relationships, and nuances in word meanings.
Activity 2: Noun-Making Suffixes: Transforming Adjective and Verbs into Nouns, p. 11	L.1	Demonstrate command of the conventions of standard English grammar and usage when writing or speaking.
	L.4	Determine or clarify the meaning of unknown and multiple-meaning words and phrases by using context clues, analyzing meaningful word parts, and consulting general and specialized reference materials, as appropriate.

Classroom Application		*Anchor Standards for English Language Arts, Grades K–12*
Phrasal Verbs, p. 13	W.1	Write arguments to support claims in an analysis of substantive topics or texts, using valid reasoning and relevant and sufficient evidence.
	W.2	Write informative/explanatory texts to examine and convey complex ideas and information clearly and accurately through the effective selection, organization, and analysis of content.
	SL.6	Adapt speech to a variety of contexts and communicative tasks, demonstrating command of formal English when indicated or appropriate.
	L.1	Demonstrate command of the conventions of standard English grammar and usage when writing or speaking.
	L.3	Apply knowledge of language to understand how language functions in different contexts, to make effective choices for meaning or style, and to comprehend more fully when reading or listening.
Connotations, p. 15	SL.1	Prepare for and participate effectively in a range of conversations and collaborations with diverse partners, building on other's ideas and expressing their own clearly and persuasively.
	SL.4	Present information, findings, and supporting evidence such that listeners can follow the line of reasoning and the organization, development, and style are appropriate to task, purpose, and audience.
	SL.6	Adapt speech to a variety of contexts and communicative tasks, demonstrating command of formal English when indicated or appropriate.

Classroom Application		Anchor Standards for English Language Arts, Grades K–12
	L.3	Apply knowledge of language to understand how language functions in different contexts, to make effective choices for meaning or style, and to comprehend more fully when reading or listening.
	L.5	Demonstrate understanding of figurative language, word relationships, and nuances in word meanings.
Register, p. 16	R.4	Interpret words and phrases as they are used in a text, including determining technical, connotative, and figurative meanings, and analyze how specific word choices shape meaning or tone.
	W.6	Use technology, including the Internet, to produce and publish writing and to interact and collaborate with others.
	W.10	Write routinely over extended time frames (time for research, reflection, and revision) and shorter time frames (a single sitting or a day or two) for a range of tasks, purposes, and audiences.
	SL.1	Prepare for and participate effectively in a range of conversations and collaborations with diverse partners, building on other's ideas and expressing their own clearly and persuasively.
	SL.6	Adapt speech to a variety of contexts and communicative tasks, demonstrating command of formal English when indicated or appropriate.
	L.3	Apply knowledge of language to understand how language functions in different contexts, to make effective choices for meaning or style, and to comprehend more fully when reading or listening.

Classroom Application		*Anchor Standards for English Language Arts, Grades K–12*
	L.4	Determine or clarify the meaning of unknown and multiple-meaning words and phrases by using context clues, analyzing meaningful word parts, and consulting general and specialized reference materials, as appropriate.
Idioms, p. 17	L.4	Determine or clarify the meaning of unknown and multiple-meaning words and phrases by using context clues, analyzing meaningful word parts, and consulting general and specialized reference materials, as appropriate.
	L.5	Demonstrate understanding of figurative language, word relationships, and nuances in word meanings.
Opposites, p. 18	L.5	Demonstrate understanding of figurative language, word relationships, and nuances in word meanings.
Gender, p. 18	R.4	Interpret words and phrases as they are used in a text, including determining technical, connotative, and figurative meanings, and analyze how specific word choices shape meaning or tone.
Intentions, p. 18	R.4	Interpret words and phrases as they are used in a text, including determining technical, connotative, and figurative meanings, and analyze how specific word choices shape meaning or tone.
	SL.6	Adapt speech to a variety of contexts and communicative tasks, demonstrating command of formal English when indicated or appropriate.
	L.3	Apply knowledge of language to understand how language functions in different contexts, to make effective choices for meaning or style, and to comprehend more fully when reading or listening.

Classroom Application		Anchor Standards for English Language Arts, Grades K–12
Chapter 3		
Classify, p. 28	SL.4	Present information, findings, and supporting evidence such that listeners can follow the line of reasoning and the organization, development, and style are appropriate to task, purpose, and audience.
	SL.5	Make strategic use of digital media and visual displays of data to express information and enhance understanding of presentations.
	L.6	Acquire and use accurately a range of general academic and domain-specific words and phrases sufficient for reading, writing, speaking, and listening at the college and career readiness level; demonstrate independence in gathering vocabulary knowledge when encountering an unknown term important to comprehension or expression.
Build, p. 28	W.10	Write routinely over extended time frames (time for research, reflection, and revision) and shorter time frames (a single sitting or a day or two) for a range of tasks, purposes, and audiences.
	L.1	Demonstrate command of the conventions of standard English grammar and usage when writing or speaking.
	L.6	Acquire and use accurately a range of general academic and domain-specific words and phrases sufficient for reading, writing, speaking, and listening at the college and career readiness level; demonstrate independence in gathering vocabulary knowledge when encountering an unknown term important to comprehension or expression.

Classroom Application		*Anchor Standards for English Language Arts, Grades K–12*
Analyze, p. 28	L.2	Demonstrate command of the conventions of standard English capitalization, punctuation, and spelling when writing.
	L.4	Determine or clarify the meaning of unknown and multiple-meaning words and phrases by using context clues, analyzing meaningful word parts, and consulting general and specialized reference materials, as appropriate.
Discern, p. 31	L.3	Apply knowledge of language to understand how language functions in different contexts, to make effective choices for meaning or style, and to comprehend more fully when reading or listening.
	L.6	Acquire and use accurately a range of general academic and domain-specific words and phrases sufficient for reading, writing, speaking, and listening at the college and career readiness level; demonstrate independence in gathering vocabulary knowledge when encountering an unknown term important to comprehension or expression.
Chapter 4		
Helping Students to Understand the Difference Between Their Receptive and Productive Vocabularies, p. 36	W.7	Conduct short as well as more sustained research projects based on focused questions, demonstrating understanding of the subject under investigation.
	W.10	Write routinely over extended time frames (time for research, reflection, and revision) and shorter time frames (a single sitting or a day or two) for a range of tasks, purposes, and audiences.

Classroom Application		Anchor Standards for English Language Arts, Grades K–12
	SL.1	Prepare for and participate effectively in a range of conversations and collaborations with diverse partners, building on other's ideas and expressing their own clearly and persuasively.
	SL.5	Make strategic use of digital media and visual displays of data to express information and enhance understanding of presentations.
	L.1	Demonstrate command of the conventions of standard English grammar and usage when writing or speaking.
	L.4	Determine or clarify the meaning of unknown and multiple-meaning words and phrases by using context clues, analyzing meaningful word parts, and consulting general and specialized reference materials, as appropriate.
	L.6	Acquire and use accurately a range of general academic and domain-specific words and phrases sufficient for reading, writing, speaking, and listening at the college and career readiness level; demonstrate independence in gathering vocabulary knowledge when encountering an unknown term important to comprehension or expression.
Keyword Groups, p. 43	R.4	Interpret words and phrases as they are used in a text, including determining technical, connotative, and figurative meanings, and analyze how specific word choices shape meaning or tone.
	L.1	Demonstrate command of the conventions of standard English grammar and usage when writing or speaking.

Classroom Application		*Anchor Standards for English Language Arts, Grades K–12*
	L.4	Determine or clarify the meaning of unknown and multiple-meaning words and phrases by using context clues, analyzing meaningful word parts, and consulting general and specialized reference materials, as appropriate.
	L.5	Demonstrate understanding of figurative language, word relationships, and nuances in word meanings.
	L.6	Acquire and use accurately a range of general academic and domain-specific words and phrases sufficient for reading, writing, speaking, and listening at the college and career readiness level; demonstrate independence in gathering vocabulary knowledge when encountering an unknown term important to comprehension or expression.
Chapter 5		
Collocations, p. 53	L.1	Demonstrate command of the conventions of standard English grammar and usage when writing or speaking.
Chapter 6		
Concept Map, p. 58	R.4	Interpret words and phrases as they are used in a text, including determining technical, connotative, and figurative meanings, and analyze how specific word choices shape meaning or tone.
Choral Reading to Nurture Fluency, p. 60	R.4	Interpret words and phrases as they are used in a text, including determining technical, connotative, and figurative meanings, and analyze how specific word choices shape meaning or tone.

Classroom Application		Anchor Standards for English Language Arts, Grades K–12
	SL.1	Prepare for and participate effectively in a range of conversations and collaborations with diverse partners, building on other's ideas and expressing their own clearly and persuasively.
Think-Pair-Share, p. 64	SL.1	Prepare for and participate effectively in a range of conversations and collaborations with diverse partners, building on other's ideas and expressing their own clearly and persuasively.
	L.2	Demonstrate command of the conventions of standard English capitalization, punctuation, and spelling when writing.
	L.4	Determine or clarify the meaning of unknown and multiple-meaning words and phrases by using context clues, analyzing meaningful word parts, and consulting general and specialized reference materials, as appropriate.
	L.5	Demonstrate understanding of figurative language, word relationships, and nuances in word meanings.
Graphic Organizers, p. 64	L.5	Demonstrate understanding of figurative language, word relationships, and nuances in word meanings.
	L.6	Acquire and use accurately a range of general academic and domain-specific words and phrases sufficient for reading, writing, speaking, and listening at the college and career readiness level; demonstrate independence in gathering vocabulary knowledge when encountering an unknown term important to comprehension or expression.
Vocabulary Games, Puzzles, Wordplay, p. 65	SL.1	Prepare for and participate effectively in a range of conversations and collaborations with diverse partners, building on other's ideas and expressing their own clearly and persuasively.

Classroom Application		*Anchor Standards for English Language Arts, Grades K–12*
	L.2	Demonstrate command of the conventions of standard English capitalization, punctuation, and spelling when writing.
	L.3	Apply knowledge of language to understand how language functions in different contexts, to make effective choices for meaning or style, and to comprehend more fully when reading or listening.
	L.5	Demonstrate understanding of figurative language, word relationships, and nuances in word meanings.
	L.6	Acquire and use accurately a range of general academic and domain-specific words and phrases sufficient for reading, writing, speaking, and listening at the college and career readiness level; demonstrate independence in gathering vocabulary knowledge when encountering an unknown term important to comprehension or expression.
Chapter 7		
Depth of Processing Exercise, p. 70	W.10	Write routinely over extended time frames (time for research, reflection, and revision) and shorter time frames (a single sitting or a day or two) for a range of tasks, purposes, and audiences.
	SL.2	Integrate and evaluate information presented in diverse media and formats, including visually, quantitatively, and orally.
	L.4	Determine or clarify the meaning of unknown and multiple-meaning words and phrases by using context clues, analyzing meaningful word parts, and consulting general and specialized reference materials, as appropriate.

Classroom Application		Anchor Standards for English Language Arts, Grades K–12
	L.5	Demonstrate understanding of figurative language, word relationships, and nuances in word meanings.
	L.6	Acquire and use accurately a range of general academic and domain-specific words and phrases sufficient for reading, writing, speaking, and listening at the college and career readiness level; demonstrate independence in gathering vocabulary knowledge when encountering an unknown term important to comprehension or expression.
Chapter 8		
Context Clues, p. 87	L.4	Determine or clarify the meaning of unknown and multiple-meaning words and phrases by using context clues, analyzing meaningful word parts, and consulting general and specialized reference materials, as appropriate.
	SL.1	Prepare for and participate effectively in a range of conversations and collaborations with diverse partners, building on other's ideas and expressing their own clearly and persuasively.
	SL.5	Make strategic use of digital media and visual displays of data to express information and enhance understanding of presentations.
Appendix G		
Morphology Charts, p. 130	L.1	Demonstrate command of the conventions of standard English grammar and usage when writing or speaking.
	L.4	Determine or clarify the meaning of unknown and multiple-meaning words and phrases by using context clues, analyzing meaningful word parts, and consulting general and specialized reference materials, as appropriate.

Classroom Application		*Anchor Standards for English Language Arts, Grades K–12*
Blogs, p. 130	W.6	Use technology, including the Internet, to produce and publish writing and to interact and collaborate with others.
	W.10	Write routinely over extended time frames (time for research, reflection, and revision) and shorter time frames (a single sitting or a day or two) for a range of tasks, purposes, and audiences.
	L.6	Acquire and use accurately a range of general academic and domain-specific words and phrases sufficient for reading, writing, speaking, and listening at the college and career readiness level; demonstrate independence in gathering vocabulary knowledge when encountering an unknown term important to comprehension or expression.
Word Games and Puzzles, p. 130	L.2	Demonstrate command of the conventions of standard English capitalization, punctuation, and spelling when writing.
	L.4	Determine or clarify the meaning of unknown and multiple-meaning words and phrases by using context clues, analyzing meaningful word parts, and consulting general and specialized reference materials, as appropriate.
Skits, p. 130	W.6	Use technology, including the Internet, to produce and publish writing and to interact and collaborate with others.
	SL.1	Prepare for and participate effectively in a range of conversations and collaborations with diverse partners, building on other's ideas and expressing their own clearly and persuasively.

Classroom Application		Anchor Standards for English Language Arts, Grades K–12
	SL.4	Present information, findings, and supporting evidence such that listeners can follow the line of reasoning and the organization, development, and style are appropriate to task, purpose, and audience.
	SL.6	Adapt speech to a variety of contexts and communicative tasks, demonstrating command of formal English when indicated or appropriate.
	L.6	Acquire and use accurately a range of general academic and domain-specific words and phrases sufficient for reading, writing, speaking, and listening at the college and career readiness level; demonstrate independence in gathering vocabulary knowledge when encountering an unknown term important to comprehension or expression.
Posters, p. 130	SL.5	Make strategic use of digital media and visual displays of data to express information and enhance understanding of presentations.
	L.4	Determine or clarify the meaning of unknown and multiple-meaning words and phrases by using context clues, analyzing meaningful word parts, and consulting general and specialized reference materials, as appropriate.
	L.5	Demonstrate understanding of figurative language, word relationships, and nuances in word meanings.
Care and Feeding of the Personal Word Journal, p. 130	W.10	Write routinely over extended time frames (time for research, reflection, and revision) and shorter time frames (a single sitting or a day or two) for a range of tasks, purposes, and audiences.

Classroom Application	*Anchor Standards for English Language Arts, Grades K–12*
	L.6 Acquire and use accurately a range of general academic and domain-specific words and phrases sufficient for reading, writing, speaking, and listening at the college and career readiness level; demonstrate independence in gathering vocabulary knowledge when encountering an unknown term important to comprehension or expression.

Works Cited

Allen, Janet. (1999). *Words, words, words: Teaching vocabulary in grades 4–12.* York, ME: Stenhouse.

Anderson, Richard C. (1977). The notion of schemata and the educational enterprise: General discussion of the conference. In *Schooling and the Acquisition of Knowledge,* edited by Richard C. Anderson, Rand J. Spiro, and William E. Montague. Hillsdale, NJ: Erlbaum, 174–189.

Baumann, James F., & Kameenui, Edward J. (1993). Research on vocabulary instruction: Ode to Voltaire. In *Handbook of Research on Teaching the English Language Arts,* edited by James Flood, Diane Lapp, James R. Squire, and Julie Jensen. New York: Macmillan, 604–632.

Benjamin, Amy. (2008). *Formative assessment for English language arts.* Larchmont, NY: Eye On Education.

Clark, Josh. (2008, September 2). "Why do people blush?" *How Stuff Works.* HowStuffWorks, Inc. 1998–2008. Available at: http://science.howstuffworks.com/blush.htm.

Craik, Fergus I.M., & Tulving, Endel. (1975). Depth of processing and the retention of words in episodic memory. *Journal of Experimental Psychology: General, 104,* 268–294.

Crovitz, Darren, & Miller, Jessica A. (2008). Register and charge: Using synonym maps to explore connotation. *English Journal, 97*(4), 49–55.

Coxhead, Averil. (2000). A new academic word list. *TESOL Quarterly, 34*(2), 213–238.

Echevarria, Mary, Vogt, Ellen, & Short, Deborah J. (2008). *Making Content Comprehensible for English Learners: The SIOP Model,* 3rd ed. Boston: Allyn and Bacon.

Farley, Mary Jane, & Elmore, Patricia B. (1992). The relationship of reading comprehension to critical thinking skills, cognitive ability, and vocabulary for a sample of underachieving college freshmen. *Educational and Psychological Measurement, 52*(4), 921–931.

Fisher, Douglas, & Frey, Nancy. (2008). *Word wise & content rich: Five essential steps to teaching academic vocabulary.* Portsmouth, NH: Heinemann.

Garner, Bette K. (2007). *Getting to got it! Helping struggling students learn how to learn.* Alexandria, VA: ASCD.

Irving, Washington. (1999). *The Legend of Sleepy Hollow.* New York: Grosset & Dunlap.

Jacobs, Heidi Hayes. (2006). *Active literacy across the curriculum: Strategies for reading, writing, speaking and listening.* Larchmont, NY: Eye On Education.

Jensen, Eric. (2000). *Brain-based learning.* San Diego, CA: The Brain Store.

Krashen, Stephen D. (2004). *The power of reading: Insights from the research,* 2nd ed. Portsmouth, NH: Heinemann.

Krashen, Stephen D. (2003). *Explorations in language acquisition and use.* Portsmouth, NH: Heinemann.

Krashen, Stephen D. (1999). *Three arguments against whole language & why they are wrong.* Portsmouth, NH: Heinemann.

Lowry, Lois. (2006). *The giver.* New York: Delacorte Press.

Marzano, Robert J. (2004). *Building background knowledge for academic achievement: Research on what works in schools.* Alexandria, VA: ASCD.

Na, Liu, & Nation, I. S. P. (1985). Factors affecting guessing vocabulary in context. *RELC Journal, 16*(1), 33–42.

Nagy, William E. (1988). *Teaching vocabulary to improve reading comprehension.* Newark, NJ: IRA.

New York Times Newspaper in education curriculum guide: A teacher's guide to the language arts. (1997). New York: New York Times, 44.

Rosch, Elanor. (1975). Cognitive representations of semantic categories. *Journal of Experimental Psychology: General, 14,* 192–233.

Rogers, T. B., Kuipers, N. A., & Kirker, W. S. (1977). Self-reference and the encoding of personal information. *Journal of Personality and Social Psychology, 35,* 677–688.

Vaishnav, Anand. (2005, September 1). Middle ground: Shattuck professor Catherine Snow's project on adolescent literacy. *Harvard Graduate School of Education: News Features & Releases.* Available at: http://www.gse.harvard.edu/news_events/features/2005/10/snow. html. Retrieved January 11, 2009.

Sousa, David A. (2001). *How the brain learns,* 2nd ed. Thousand Oaks, CA: Corwin.

Twain, Mark. (1999). *Puddin'head Wilson.* North Chelmsford, MA: Courier Dover Publications.

Vygotsky, L. S. (1962). *Thought and Language.* Cambridge, MA: MIT Press.

Zimmer, Benjamin. (2008, April 23) "GHOTI" before Shaw. Available at: http://languagelog.ldc.upenn.edu/nll/?p=81. Retrieved August 20, 2008.

Zwier, Lawrence J. (2002). *Building academic vocabulary.* Michigan Series in English for Academic & Professional Purposes. Ann Arbor: University of Michigan Press.